GREG DYKE
My Part in his Downfall

By the same author:

Trench Fever (Little, Brown, 1998)
Roger, Sausage & Whippet (Headline, 2012)

Forthcoming
The Hoarse Oaths of Fife (Sept 2015)

GREG DYKE
My Part in his Downfall

Chris Moore

Days and Awaydays in BBC News
2001 – 2004

Universe Press

Universe Press
an imprint of Unicorn Publishing Group
66 Charlotte Street
London W1T 4QE

A catalogue record for this book is available from
the British Library

Second edition

Paperback ISBN 978-0-9932424-0-3
EPub ISBN 978-0-9932424-2-7
PDF ISBN 978-0-9932424-3-4

Cover design by Ryan Gearing
Typeset by Vivian@Bookscribe

Printed and bound in the UK by Berforts, Stevenage

PREQUEL

It starts in Bush House, London WC2. Anyone strolling down Kingsway from the Bloomsbury direction soon becomes aware of Bush House looming over the trees at the end of the boulevard. Looking down on the red buses and black taxis stand two titans of stone personifying the British Empire and the United States of America. Between them they hold a flaming torch, symbolic of their shared duty towards a world exhausted by the Great War of 1914–1918. Bush House was named after an American property developer who conceived it as a temple to the healing effects of trans-Atlantic commerce. Eighty years on, in the winter of the year 2001, the names of Mr Bush's first tenants are still discernible as ghostly stains on his walls; all have been replaced by today's single tenant, the World Service of the British Broadcasting Corporation.

It is possible you've heard of the BBC World Service. Measured by the size of its regular audience, 153 million listeners, it is one of the bigger international radio stations and some say the best. More than 1000 people work inside Bush House, gathering news, checking news and translating it into 43 languages for transmission around the world 24 hours a day. At the centre of this activity is the Newsroom on the Fourth Floor of South East Wing. At the heart of the Newsroom is Centre Desk, where I am hard at it when the phone rings. The Editor wants to see me for what is known in BBC News as an honest conversation – one where the person behind the desk doesn't much admire the person sitting in front of it.

The Editor's management suite is on the Third Floor of South East Wing, which was once the domain of World Service Current Affairs. Several re-organisations ago World Service Current Affairs and the World Service Newsroom were merged into one department, World Service News & Current Affairs, WSNCA. Since then the friendly rivalry that used to exist between the Third and Fourth Floors has curdled into a less friendly one.

Our soon-to-be-departed Editor gestures me to sit. John Morrison was despatched to Bush House from BBC News HQ at Television Centre, London W12, with a brief to fix the budget and clear out the dead wood. The Newsroom veterans who ran WSNCA were replaced by a *nouveau* generation from Current Affairs with no allegiance to the previous dispensation – a way of doing things that prospered under John Birt, the BBC Director-General who decided that World Service journalists didn't properly belong to the World Service but could be much more usefully administered by BBC News in Telly Centre. The current Director-General, Greg Dyke, has found it expedient not to return to the more sensible prior arrangement. That's why we now have to answer to two sets of bosses – the BBC News junta at Telly Centre plus our own World Service hierarchs in Centre Block*. With twice as many bosses to please it's getting harder not to displease someone or other.

The Managing Director of the BBC World Service in the winter of 2001 is a man called Mark Byford. A couple of weeks ago someone working for Mark plastered the interior of Bush House with posters of celebrity businessmen, politicians and media stars praising the World Service for its influence for good in the world.

You might think that with 153 million listeners there is no need for boasting about our place in their esteem which is why, a few days ago, I wrote a note in the Talkback* section of the Newsroom Log*. I suggested that perhaps the ulterior motive for spending public money on strictly internal propaganda was to show any visitors from the Foreign Office, which funds the World Service to the tune of nearly £200 million per year, how eager we are to embrace the New Labour government's 'Cool Britannia' campaign.

"Do you know," says John, sliding across his desk a printed-off copy of my note, "do you know how embarrassing it is for me to find one of my senior journalists writing this kind of thing? It sets a very bad tone for the department. I am personally very disappointed in your attitude. I have to tell you, Chris, that this is a very career-limiting thing to do …"

To make quite sure that I have got the message John leans forward to look me in the eye.

"This. Is a very. Career-limiting. Thing. To do."

The view from John's corner office consists of rows of blank, inscrutable windows looking down into the inner courtyard used as the Bush House car park. Our colleagues from ex-Communist countries are familiar with architecture built to project power and enforce conformity. One of them, Georgi Markov, left this building on 7 September 1978, and was assassinated. Someone poisoned him with a toxic pellet shot from an umbrella while he was crossing Waterloo Bridge which is why, to this day, some of our European colleagues feel safer broadcasting under assumed names when speaking truth to power.

"Two things, John. One: I am entitled to an honest opinion about how this organisation is managed and I am entitled to express it in Talkback because that's what Talkback is for. Second thing: Do you really think it's a good use of your taxes to stick posters of the Dalai Lama all over the Bush House canteen?"

John shuffles the papers on his desk.

"When I first arrived here," he says, "you were one of the people who was described to me as a bit of a disappointment. There's a feeling that you have not delivered on your potential."

Potential is a BBC code word for promotability. In the BBC we are expected to show our suitability for promotion by acting like a boss in order to become one. One reason I have not delivered on my potential is because I do not want spend my days like John – shuffling papers and wearing cufflinks in a corner office while all the exciting stuff is happening elsewhere. I am a lifer. I love the toil. The Bush House Newsroom is the only place in BBC News where people are paid to put events into written form only, the essential function of the journalist. The Newsroom I joined was a shrine to good writing in clear English fit for translation into any language. Where else would I want to work in these interesting times? Watching John's face as he tries to stare me down I realise that Bush House is threatened from within, and I don't like the look of that at all.

* *BBC jargon and slang marked with an asterisk is explained in the glossary at the back.*

CHAPTER ONE

Hey! Who Killed the Bulletin?

Wednesday, 5 December 2001. Law Society Hall, Chancery Lane, London WC1. Welcome to the first WSNCA Band 10 Awayday of the new era. A Band 10 is a journalist like me, a Senior Duty Editor on Band 10 of the BBC pay scale, the topmost stratum of which is Band 11. An Awayday is the properly constituted channel through which the bosses of BBC News transmit their ideas to those further down the food chain in order to foment blue-sky thinking. Chairing the proceedings today is Mary Hockaday, the erstwhile Current Affairs producer chosen to be WSNCA's next Editor instead of John Morrison.

Mary is big news in our little world. She is the first female Editor of the department and the first Current Affairs producer to get the job. Her appointment signals a dynamic, changeful shift in the climate. The allegiance of our previous leadership was to the methods and manners of Bush House rather than BBC News. It is otherwise with Mary and her team. Their careers will be influenced henceforth by how they are perceived by the Alpha primates at Telly Centre; it's thanks to them that Mary & Co. are no longer paid according to their grade on the pay scale but according to the system of incentivised contractual rewards known as 'SPS', Special Personal Salary. Some invoke a gulf in understanding, others a glass ceiling, but whatever the metaphor our new bosses are now firmly on the side of the

BBC divide separating those with private health insurance and car allowances from those who cycle in to work with their lunch in a sandwich box.

Mary opens the Awayday by introducing the Head of BBC Radio News, Stephen Mitchell. He addresses us from a seated position at the head of the conference table. He says he's not going to stand because he was out late last night and is getting too old for it. And he can't stay long because he's got to go to a meeting with the Director-General, Greg Dyke, about the Oryx case.

Greg has spent his first couple of years in the job not paying any obvious attention to BBC News. But the Oryx case, which involves a horrendous libel perpetrated by the geniuses of Telly Centre, doesn't give him much of a choice because the Director-General of the BBC is also its Editor-in-Chief. Sorting out the mess, according to Steve Mitchell, is going to cost a lot. In the meantime, he wants us to know that he is very pleased to have Mary as his new Editor at World Service News & Current Affairs. There was a very strong field of applicants for John Morrison's job from inside and outside the BBC and we should feel pleased that World Service was able to attract so many high calibre candidates.

The high calibre candidate wanted most hopefully by the Band 10 editors in the Newsroom was any friendly, reliable, experienced broadcaster with a sharp nose for news. But there had been signs all along. Greg Dyke is a declared champion of Diversity. When he looked around the room during his official Christmas dinner and saw too many blokes and mainly white faces he knew something was wrong. He has now set course for change with a capital C.

'Experienced' and 'reliable' are no longer boxes that need to be ticked. Change is preferable to no-Change and the sooner the better. So that's what we've got.

Mary opens her PowerPoint presentation by saying she was absolutely "bowled over" to get the job and feels "very proud". She tells us that we have been through some huge changes with John Morrison and there'll be more of them now she's in charge. The World Service has set itself a target to increase its global audience next year from 153 million listeners a week to 155 million listeners. We in WSNCA will be expected to play our part by modernising our sound while retaining the authority of our journalism. Mary also wants "high impact" journalism, by which she seems to mean programmes that will win prizes and get us written about in *The Guardian*. We should not be shy, she says, about being so good.

When Mary sits down Steve Mitchell glides silently from the room and John Morrison rises to deliver his valedictory speech. It is one of those occasions when the shorthand I learned as a trainee BBC journalist still comes in handy.

"Heading into retirement is a slightly odd process," says John. "Gradually you become invisible … While you're in this process of fading away people sidle up to you in the corridor and say, 'What do you want as your leaving present?' And you think, 'How much are they thinking of – a pint of lager or a case of Chateau Lafitte?' "

He says he doesn't care what present we give him, so long as it reminds him of us.

"In the case of Phil Harding," he says, "that would be his flannel. Or in Mark Damazer's case a four-minute seminar on the latest proposals for an Afghan peace settlement delivered in one unbroken sentence."

After two-and-a-half years in his corner office, John says he has come up with a "big thought" as a gift of his own by which we can remember him.

"And my big thought is this – cheer up! There's something in the water that seems to make you think there's a conspiracy afoot to denigrate World Service. You seem to think you're not quite as good as everyone else in the BBC. Well, you are *wrong* ..."

John tells us he has never, ever, come across such a talented group of journalists. With an average of about 15 years BBC experience per person the Band 10s of WSNCA comprise "an amazing editorial entity." He says there is nothing like us anywhere else in BBC News. We are the best bit of the best news organisation in the world.

"Your audience love what you do," he says. "For many of them what you do is as necessary to life as food and air and water – and there are very few people who can say that about their work. So cheer up. Ahead lie the sunlit uplands. Relax. Enjoy it."

John's speech sounds like something drafted for a far more exalted audience than us lot, sitting with our arms folded, gasping for the coffee to arrive. He never did get to grips with matching all of our names and faces to our rota initials so it's not surprising that none of us is mentioned in his speech. He was sent to turn our world upside down and now that's done he's galloping for the hills like a *bandido* with his saddlebags full of swag bouncing behind him. If our new Editor has ever edited a radio news bulletin for the World Service or anyone else none of us is aware of it. From now on it will be down to the Newsroom's Band 10s to keep the show on the road. Thanks, John. *Hasta la vista!* Thanks for the leadership.

⊷━◦━◅

Tuesday, 5 February 2002. Newsroom, Centre Desk. The lease on Bush House is approaching expiry and the committee of BBC bosses appointed by Greg Dyke to discuss where next to put the World Service has reached its decision. Various schemes have been mooted in the past such as buying Bush House outright or negotiating a longer lease but it's been decided that the way forward is to prise apart the BBC's main headquarters, the venerable Broadcasting House in Portland Place, and insert us therein. I arrive for my night shift to find the marble foyer of Bush House crammed with architects' models and video screens showing how 'New Broadcasting House' will look – like a glass and steel box with knobs on. Mark Byford says it will provide exactly the right kind of spatial environment the World Service needs to launch itself into the digital age.

The grand plans of the rest of the BBC fade into due significance when viewed from Centre Desk with its panoramic 360 degree outlook on world events. With a bit of luck Greg Dyke's career as a property developer will collapse around his ears and we'll be able to stay in our Bush House fortress for a few more years yet. What's vexing Centre Desk is the current state of the overnight tea trolley. Drastic cuts in provision have been imposed without consultation. We analyse the trolley's contents for the purpose of writing an accurate message in the Newsroom Log. A fair and equitable division of the food and drink supplied for the 20 staff on duty in the Newsroom tonight provides a ration, per person, as follows: one tea bag or sachet of Nescafe; half a cheese portion plus half a cracker; one bite of a Danish pastry; a shared nibble of a piece of fruit.

This is not quite the 'management of change' we were promised the last time we went on strike to improve conditions on the night shift. Centre Desk's sworn allegiance is to our listeners *via* a computer software package known as the Electronic News Production System, ENPS*. Our task each shift, day or night, is to download news from one part of ENPS and smelt it into the form of news bulletins in another. To do this for ten-and-a-half hours while the rest of the BBC is tucked up in bed and dreaming its dreams the Newsroom needs caffeine and calories. Not that we're whingeing. Greg Dyke has declared war on whingers.

'Whingeing BBC staff will be shown the yellow card if they are caught making negative remarks about the corporation,' says the *Daily Mail*. 'Director General Greg Dyke, a keen football fan and former director of Manchester United, hopes the idea will marginalise what he calls "the cynics and moaners". In an extraordinary address to mark his second year in office, he told his 20,000 staff the BBC was seen as "safe, arrogant and out of touch" by both employees and viewers … Mr Dyke said he had a yellow card with the words "Cut the crap and make it happen" printed on it . "I plan to bring it out at every meeting when someone is trying to stop a good idea rather than make it happen," he added.'

The *Independent* puts Greg's personal worth at 15 million quid.

'He wants colour; he wants excitement; he wants risk-taking. What he doesn't want is a sensible, institutional carpet …'

Centre Desk groans in weary disbelief.

" 'Sensible *carpet*'?"

Mark Byford is not the kind of corporate leader to restrain himself when called upon to endorse the party line on floor coverings, or anything else.

' ... I hope everyone has been able to read or see Greg's address *One BBC: Making it Happen*. It involves all of us, you and me, all of our colleagues in our teams, all of us in the World Service ... It's our opportunity to make the BBC a better place ... It's about inspiring *creativity* in everything we do ... It's about *living* the values of the BBC all the time ... It's about reducing bureaucracy and making the place a *can do* culture ... It's about *leading* more and managing less ... It's about ensuring our *work spaces* stimulate creativity ... It should be a lot of fun and it's so appropriate and timely. I'm really enthusiastic about it ...'

The average corporate employee can only take so much of this kind of talk before *losing faith*. But anyone who chooses to remember aloud that Greg was appointed Director-General of the BBC after giving the Labour Party a chunky cash donation is branded a whinger

"If he's so keen on valuing people why doesn't he give us a decent trolley? Eh?"

At the end of my shift, heading into the cold, grey dawn, I pause in the foyer for another inspection of the architect's model of New Broadcasting House. It reminds me again of the iron rule: Change always ends badly at the BBC, especially if it's got anything to do with new buildings, new technology ... or people.

Friday, 8 February. Newsroom, Centre Desk. Last night shift of four. The headlines when our team takes over Centre Desk are: Taleban prisoners at Guantanamo Bay; Israeli Prime Minister in Washington for talks; China faces a crisis of rural unemployment. The headlines when we leave are: Olympic Chief declares war on drug cheats; President Bush warns Yasser Arafat over Middle East violence; street protests in Venezuela. That's showbiz. As soon as we have installed the Olympics as our lead story I catch up with Newsroom Log. Our new Editor has given birth.

'Mary's Baby. Mary and Sara are the proud and delighted parents of a baby girl. No name as yet. She was born on Sunday morning weighing in at a wacking [sic] 9lb 4 ozs. Mother and baby in good health.'

›‹•›‹•›‹

Friday, 22 February. Newsroom, Centre Desk. The half-term break was hell. It is sheer relief to get back to the smelly old day job – until I check my e-mails.

FROM: Greg Dyke.
TO: All staff.

'By the time you read this I'll be lying on a beach in Barbados (groans all round) so to cheer you all up I thought I'd update you on what's happened in the ten days since we launched "One BBC – Making It Happen" … The response has been brilliant … we've even started playing our radio stations in the lifts at Broadcasting House … As I've walked around the BBC this week, and tell me if I'm imagining it, I've certainly felt a new buzz around the place … Yours, Greg.'

The latest news on the architectural work-in-progress now known officially as 'New BH' is that the BBC has made a mess of its planning application. Westminster City Council is upset that the design for Greg's *Krudpalast* will block protected views of the Houses of Parliament from Primrose Hill. The planners are also reported to be unhappy with the proposed new building's glass façade, preferring something a little less showy in Portland stone. *The Times* says that when the BBC team heard this they threw a tantrum and threatened to call in their New Labour contacts to get their plans pushed through.

Sunday, 10 March. Newsroom, Centre Desk. Without the newspapers no one on the BBC pay scale would have a clue what was going on at the SPS level. According to *The Mail on Sunday*, Greg Dyke and his mates have splurged £250,000 on their latest Awayday.

'… As BBC staff waited for buses and paid for their own tea and biscuits, the Director General and key members of his 'Make It Happen' team stayed at the exclusive Mansion on Turtle Creek hotel in Dallas where suites cost £1,750 a night. The six day junket taking him to Dallas and San Francisco was organised by London-based "creative and innovation" training company What If and is marketed under the title "Top Dog" …'

Tuesday, 12 March. Newsroom Band 10s Awayday, Law Society Hall. The main item on the agenda today is the future of the Newsroom's straight-read bulletin, the oldest and simplest method of presenting news on radio.

For decades the straight-read bulletin at the World Service was virtually the only thing produced in the Newsroom. There was one kind of bulletin and one only and it lasted nine minutes and 15 seconds. The hundreds of translators scattered around Bush House had to translate it word for word. The only other thing the Newsroom produced was a programme of 15 minutes duration called *Radio Newsreel* which consisted of correspondents' despatches, one after the other. When the *Reel* got the hatchet in the 1980s it was replaced by a half-hour programme called *Newsdesk,* whose future now looks similarly bleak. In the days when the 'dead wood' supplied the leadership, the Newsroom's job was to set the agenda and the rest of Bush House, including the Third Floor, followed its lead. Since the *bouleversement* effected by John Morrison, the new head honcho in the Newsroom is a former Current Affairs editor called Steve Titherington, whose official job title is Editor, Core News.

Sometimes, what with all the testosterone and career rivalry fizzing around, life in Core News can feel a bit like a rehearsal for a low-budget sitcom. Steve is not the only character prone to outbursts of self-dramatisation but he does seem to need attention more than most. Tithers, sometimes also known as 'the Tith', is shaping up to be the type of boss known in BBC News as a strong personality. On the Third Floor he was a staunch believer in the divine right of Current Affairs editors to ignore Newsroom thinking at will. But he is a shrewd cookie and he's doing his best to make the transition. Today, he's invited his Bush House boss along as guest of honour, Phil Harding, Director of News for World Service.

"Call me Phil," he says, getting us off to a flying start.

With his grey hair, leather jacket and funky spectacle frames Phil is himself a character study of a particular BBC role model. Work should be fun, yeah. Get yourself a man bag like a Milanese hipster. Phil says he's expecting a vigorous debate this morning on the theme of straight-read bulletins *versus* illustrated bulletins, i.e. those containing audio sound-bites. His mission is to "explain my reasoning".

He begins by listing the virtues of the straight-read bulletin: it compresses more journalism into a restricted space than any other format; it is the most comprehensible way of delivering news to listeners who have English as a second or third language, which is most World Service listeners; it remains the most effective bulletin for short-wave broadcasting, which is how most of our audience receive us; and it offers a showcase for good writing, one of the most important aspects of our journalism. Journalists, newsreaders and listeners all like the straight-read bulletin. It is clear, sharp, respected and trusted. Some of our bulletins have already been illustrated and Phil thinks the time has now come for the remainder of the straight-reads to be dumped.

The straight-read format demands clarity of expression and imposes the supremacy of fact over opinion. Clarity and factual authority do not fit comfortably with the chatty, modern sound that Phil Harding and Mark Byford require in the digital age. While paying ritual respect to the World Service tradition of fairness and measured impartiality, our bosses would prefer us to sound a bit more like the American satellite channel, CNN. The code words are: warm; accessible; modern. Phil Harding says that, having done a lot of listening to the World Service since arriving in Bush House, he's decided to aim for much *warmer* sound, something with a more *modern* texture, news that's a lot more *user-friendly*.

Phil does not accept that straight-read bulletins are more comprehensible than illustrated bulletins. He does not believe that the future of the World Service lies in increasing its audience on short-wave. Short-wave broadcasting is yesterday's technology. Listeners who don't have English as their first language are yesterday's audience. They live in poor parts of the world where they don't have a choice.

What makes BBC bosses look good is delivering change and the best change of all is an increase in the size of the audience. In the case of the World Service that means less broadcasting on our short wave transmitters and more re-broadcasting *via* client FM radio stations around the world. Our news is available on FM in 130 capital cities. If more client radio outlets can be persuaded to take World Service bulletins their audiences can be counted as ours. But they want illustrated bulletins not straight-reads. The output of most FM stations is based on pop music and the advertising jingle. An illustrated bulletin with its busier sound and absence of fibre fits better with the ambience of pop music than the cool, factual tones of a British newsreader.

Last year Mark Byford did something that had hitherto been thought unthinkable for a Managing Director of the BBC World

Service, he closed down radio transmitters, those beaming news bulletins and programmes on short-wave to Australasia and North America. He flicked the switch on one of the most loyal audiences in international broadcasting in order to save £500,000 for re-investing in FM re-broadcasting.

Sometimes, often, the management of change in the BBC feels little different from the management of vandalism. Chopping our bulletins down to size and stuffing them with sound-bites is going to make them sound like gobbledegook. When we ask Phil when exactly he intends pulling the plug on the straight-read bulletin he frowns like someone steeling himself to take the tough decisions that sometimes have to be made in publicly funded institutions where nobody ever gets sacked for making the wrong call.

"Sooner rather than later," he growls toughly.

Cheers, Phil. Cool. Thanks for coming to our Awayday to explain your reasoning.

⊢─•─○─◦─⊣

Wednesday, 13 March. Newsroom, Centre Desk. As soon as I arrive for my 1130 late shift everyone on the team wants to hear the result of yesterday's Awayday. I tell them that Phil Harding has decided to kill off the straight-read bulletin but we don't know when.

"Oh yes we do," says SMJ, "they've made an announcement."

Someone prints off a copy of the letter that has been sent to World Service newsreaders.

'As you will be aware from our Awaydays over the last year we have been considering standardising the news bulletins on the network. The decision to go ahead with this has now been taken, with the illustrated bulletin being the single network bulletin. We are proposing to make this change at the beginning of May. I cannot pretend that this is a happy day ...'

CHAPTER TWO

My Beeb Race Hell

Monday, 18 March. Newsroom, Centre Desk. I bump into Sharan Sandhu in the car park while nipping out for a cup of proper coffee from the Italian café in the arcade of shops that forms the rear exit to Bush House. For the past couple of years Sharan has been pursuing a claim against the BBC for race and sex discrimination. I agreed last year to be one of her witnesses because I believe that she was indeed discriminated against. The barrister who's representing Sharan at the tribunal has just increased her fees to £3000 a day. The only reason Sharan has been able to get this far is because her solicitor husband has been working for free. Now she's wondering if she should pack it in. I ask her if she genuinely believes she was discriminated against.

"Yes."

"Do you believe you were shat on for years?"

"Yes."

"Do you believe that every BBC boss who's had anything to do with your case is a bastard?"

"Yes."

"There's your answer."

⊢⊶⊙⊷⊣

Wednesday, 20 March. Newsroom, Centre Desk. Third morning shift. Out of the house at 0645 hours for my third consecutive bike ride from London SW4 into Bush House on puddled roads dense with foggy gloom. The headlines I inherit are: Zimbabwe kicked out of Commonwealth because of last week's rigged elections (12 hours old); suicide bomber in Israel kills five people (two hours old); Tommy Suharto appears in an Indonesian court to face murder charges (who cares). Our first decision is to ditch Zimbabwe. The second is to work some American diplomacy into the Israel story (envoy Zinni to meet Arafat and Sharon for ceasefire talks) and make it the lead story for the 0900 editorial conference on the grounds that it will hold us until we can think of something clever to do with Italy.

Late last night an expert advisor working on Berlusconi's unpopular labour reforms was shot dead, apparently by the Red Brigades. Berlusconi has now warned of the return of terrorism to Italian politics. An Italian lead story would give us a complete change of sound from the news grind of the past few weeks, which has consisted almost exclusively of Zimbabwe (elections), Middle East (Palestinian suicide bombers) and Afghanistan (America's 'War on Terror'). At the 0900 editorial conference our European Affairs analyst, William Horsley, gives the Italy story strong support, which comes as a major relief since the top brains from all four corners of Bush House gather for the 0900 editorial and it can often be an ordeal. The Newsroom is full of generalists, people who take a wide view of listeners' interests and concerns. The foreign language sections of Bush House are full of specialists, steeped in detail about their particular regions of the world's news map. Woe betide any Newsroom editor who starts off the 0900 editorial conference by mis-pronouncing some African president's name or getting his Sunnis and his Shi'as in a twist.

By 1100 hours Centre Desk is chugging along nicely with a shiny new Italian story in the lead when the presenter of our Current Affairs flagship programme, *Newshour,* calls in on his mobile phone from the middle of a traffic jam. He says he's got a hot interview with the President of Nigeria, Olesegun Obasanjo, about yesterday's decision to suspend Zimbabwe from the Commonwealth. Obasanjo reckons that when he stopped in Zimbabwe on his way to London he got President Mugabe and the opposition leader, Morgan Tsvangirai, to agree to hold reconciliation talks with a view to holding a re-run of the disputed elections.

To me it sounds like a good line on yesterday's news. But this *Newshour* presenter is not just any old *Newshour* presenter, he is also a one-time *Today* presenter on Radio Four, with an ego to match. So to keep everyone happy I brief someone to listen to his interview and re-write our Zimbabwe story accordingly. Centre Desk's Duty Editor, known to the rota as CJT, approves the story when it is written, a process which requires him to change the status field on the story in the computer from red (unapproved draft story) to green (story checked, approved and fit for broadcast).

At 1220 hours our star *Newshour* presenter, who's arrived back on the Third Floor, sends me a message. Centre Desk has got the wrong angle on the Obasanjo story. He says we should be talking about Obasanjo's reconciliation plans for Mugabe and Tsvangirai. When I take my first look at the story it has a top line quoting Obasanjo as saying that the Commonwealth had no choice but to suspend Zimbabwe from membership because its election monitors say last week's election was rigged. Nothing about the alleged prospects for political reconciliation.

Fortuitously, a flash snaps up on the *Agence France Presse*, AFP, newswire: Morgan Tsvangirai has been summoned to appear in court in Harare to be charged with treason. This is obviously a better top line to the Zimbabwe story than anything Obasanjo has to say. But AFP's source is an anonymous spokesman in Tsvangirai's Movement for Democratic Change, the MDC. These guys have steered us wrong before. About three weeks ago they said Tsvangirai had been detained by the police for questioning and all they did was charge him for having an unlicensed mobile phone. So I don't trust AFP quoting the MDC. I ask the Intake desk to check it out with our bureau in Johannesburg, which is the place from where we have to report on Zimbabwe because Mugabe has banned the BBC until further notice.

Suddenly, Tithers is at my shoulder. He is looking at some notes he's made of *Newshour's* interview with Obasanjo. He says it's strong stuff. Reconciliation-leading-to-new-elections is a good strong line. *Newshour* has got us an exclusive. Maybe it's strong enough to lead the bulletin? I nod towards my computer screen.

"Or how about this – 'Tsvangirai in treason charge shock horror'?"

The Centre Desk phone rings. It is editor of *Newshour* down on the Third Floor. The Obasanjo story we've got is wrong. It doesn't have that strong reconciliation-leading-to-new-elections line. And shouldn't Zimbabwe be higher than number three in the headlines? Couldn't it be a good new lead story for the top of the next hour? I tell him that according to AFP Morgan Tsvangirai has just been summoned to face treason charges.

"And if that's true," I say, "*that's* our new top line on the Zimbabwe story. We're checking it out. In the meantime, remind your presenter that he is not paid to decide our headlines."

This puts Tithers on the spot. He is nudging me to follow the *Newshour* line on Zimbabwe at the same time that I am telling *Newshour* to follow the Newsroom's line. The only person in the room, apart from Tithers, who has listened to the whole of the Obasanjo interview is our Newsroom reporter. She gives me a couple of lines of copy* about Obasanjo and reconciliation which I personally write into the Zimbabwe story.

By about 1320 my headlines for 1400 are drafted: Italy (Berlusconi says he will defend Italian democracy against the re-emergence of political terrorism); Middle East (American envoy Zinni works for ceasefire despite latest suicide bombing); Zimbabwe (Reports say the defeated presidential candidate, Morgan Tsvangirai, has been summoned to face treason charges). I cannot announce my new headline plans on the Newsroom tannoy until Jo'burg either confirms or knocks down* AFP's Tsvangirai story. In the meantime, with a snap* story about Zimbabwe written and ready but not greened, I wander into Tithers' glass-walled corner office where he is listening to *Newshour* with his feet on the desk.

I tell him I am quite happy to lead with Zimbabwe if the Tsvangirai-treason line is confirmed. That may take one phone call to Jo'burg; it may take hours of dithering. The cops in Harare may decide to do what they did last time – charge Tsvangirai with some minor offence and let him go. Either way, we cannot lead the BBC World Service news with *Newshour's* reconciliation-leading-to-new-elections line.

❧

"Why not?"

We both know that if Tithers was still editing *Newshour* he would be trumpeting his presenter's world exclusive about Zimbabwe to the world whether the SDE on Centre Desk thought it was news or not.

"Because I don't believe it."

Mugabe is a known liar. Obasanjo is a liar's messenger. Zimbabwe is yesterday's story. Italy must stay the lead story until the new Tsvangirai-treason story is confirmed because the Italy story is still fresh, it is based on hard facts and it has developed nicely for us all morning: the Pope has expressed horror at the killing; Italian trades unions have organised work stoppages; Parliament is holding an emergency debate. Tithers tells me that I am the Senior Duty Editor and the lead story is mine to call … but it would be a shame to waste a world exclusive.

I return to my desk where my draft headlines are waiting impatiently to be greened. I check the newswires. If Tsvangirai is charged with treason, Centre Desk wins; if not, I am an arse.

Another AFP flash pops up: Tsvangirai charged with treason. The source, again, is an MDC spokesman. The same source as before? This cannot be my second independent source. Where is Reuters when you need it?

The news producer checking out our Tsvangirai-treason story in Jo'burg is called Rageh Omar. All we need is one line of copy from him. I have known Rageh since he first arrived at World Service on a training scheme. He used to help me with the fiddly bits when I was editing *Newshour* on attachment for a few ghastly months in the days before the transition from tape recorders to digital production. Where is Rageh? Where is our second source?

I tinker with our un-greened Zimbabwe snap and wait another minute, and then another.

At 1352 hours, with eight minutes to go before air-time, the News Traffic tannoy announces that Rageh Omar is on the line: Morgan Tsvangirai has been charged with treason.

I green the snap and get on the tannoy.

"*Bing-bong!* Hello, Newsroom -"

I sound ultra-calm and measured.

"Zimbabwe is the new lead story for the top of the hour. The snap's in the system. A new Top* will be with you shortly."

I check that the bulletin producer will be able to get the Rageh Omar despatch into the 1400 bulletin and re-order my headlines: Zimbabwe; Italy; Middle East. At about 1404 I finally get away from my desk for lunch. On the way out I pop into the Third Floor conference room for *Newshour*'s post-programme feedback session.

"Evening, all."

Silence. Several Current Affairs editors and producers are slumped round the table with moody expressions on their faces. They have just finished trashing me in my absence for making a mess of their Obasanjo scoop. I am about 30 seconds into the explanation of my reasoning when the presenter erupts in full *prima donna* mode.

"Why is it that the Newsroom always fucks it up, Chris? Time after time after time, whatever we do, however much of a steer we give you, the Newsroom can always be relied upon to fuck it up ..."

He thrashes the table in front of him with his scripts.

"No," I say. "The Newsroom doesn't always fuck it up. We only sometimes fuck it up."

"Your Zimbabwe story was about *election monitors*! 'President Obasanjo explains the Commonwealth's decision to suspend Zimbabwe ...' Who came up with that crap headline? The story we gave you was about *reconciliation* and the prospect of *new elections*. I told you the story and you got it wrong."

"We did not get it wrong. We didn't attribute anything to Obasanjo that he did not say. Factually speaking, we got it right. It's just that our story didn't purvey the line that you wanted. Which doesn't matter. Because the line you wanted was pure shit."

"Bollocks!"

"Within an hour of landing your so-called world exclusive about reconciliation-leading-to-new-elections, Mugabe made a mockery of it. He's charged Tsvangirai with treason. You call that reconciliation?"

"We got a world exclusive, Chris. The Newsroom is always –"

"You can call 14 minutes of Obasanjo droning on about yesterday's news a world exclusive but I bet you a month's wages – your wages, not mine – that not a single news agency will pick up your interview when they hear it because it's not news. There is no reconciliation. Tsvangirai is facing a treason charge. The Newsroom was nailing down the news while you were recycling crap. More to the point: why didn't you get to the Italy story until half-past the hour? You were 30 minutes into your programme before you got to today's lead story. And what did you give the listener when you did get to Italy? Three questions to David Willey and a 'thanks for that'. We spent all morning developing Italy as a lead story. You ignored it. Otherwise, it was a great show. Well done everybody ..."

Wednesday, 27 March. Newsroom, Centre Desk. We are lolling around at our desks, trying to stay awake at the end of our night shift when the Controller of BBC1, Lorraine Heggessy, pops up on our monitor screens. She's booked herself onto the *Breakfast* show to answer criticism of her bold, new, red-ish ideas for the on-screen BBC1 logo. Instead of a balloon gliding over beautiful chunks of British landscape the network's identity will henceforth be personified by people in wheelchairs playing basketball, dancers in red leotards and rugby players performing a Maori *haka*. Lorraine has sent an e-mail to all BBC staff explaining that the aim is to 'reflect the diversity and totality of Britain'. The *Daily Telegraph, The Sun* and the *Daily Mail* say it's another example of political correctness gone mad at the BBC.

Lorraine does look somewhat defensive, perched on the edge of her seat, but she delivers in the same perky manner that made her a favourite in BBC Journalist Training, circa 1980, when she and I used to sit next to each other. The only cringe came when the simpering presenter referred to her as 'the boss'. The BBC has always been a bastion of boss worship but it's taken Greg Dyke's ascendancy to make it compulsory.

◄─►─◦─◄─►

Monday, 15 April. Newsroom, Centre Desk. An email arrives from Stephen Mitchell, Head of Radio News.

'Dear Colleagues … An Employment Tribunal involving one of our journalists in Bush House and the BBC begins this week and may well make the newspapers in the days ahead. Sharan works as a Broadcast Journalist in the newsroom at Bush. Her case, supported by the NUJ, is that she's a victim of direct and indirect race and sex discrimination. Some of the claims made in support of her case will attract media coverage and, in the way of tribunals, evidence supporting the BBC's position comes at the end … I'll try to keep you in touch with the proceedings. I ask when you read other reports of the evidence, you read them with care and examine the motives of those doing the reporting. Stephen Mitchell.'

▸━◆━○━◆━◂

Saturday, 20 April. Newsroom, Centre Desk. One of our union reps is telling us about the Sharan Sandhu case. She says the BBC is bound to lose and will settle out of court. AC is the kind of union rep I take seriously. But how can the BBC allow the World Service to be branded as racist and not fight the charge every inch of the way?

"I'm telling you," says AC, "the BBC is absolutely going to lose this case."

Sharan has told me she doesn't think her chances are much better than fifty-fifty. Nor has her new barrister put her chances any higher.

"I've got ten quid here," I tell AC, "and it says Sharan will lose. The BBC must win this case – by hook or by crook. The BBC cannot be branded as racist, not at the World Service."

"You're on," says AC.

My own appearance before the tribunal has been set down for next week and I'm not looking forward to it.

Thursday, 25 April. Home Desk, London SW4. News flash. I am re-reading my Sharan Sandhu witness statement when the phone rings. It is Sharan's husband. My evidence will not be needed. The BBC has decided to settle out of court.

Friday, 26 April. Home Desk, London SW4. Sharan Sandhu rings. She says the BBC settled out of court because it was getting hammered in the press. Apparently, ten national and regional newspapers carried the story on the first day of evidence. When I ask how much money the BBC has given her to settle out of court, she says she can't tell me because she's signed a confidentiality agreement.

"Go on, I'm one of your star witnesses."

"I can't."

"Yes you can."

"No I can't"

All she will say is that *The Independent*'s report of a payment of £50,000 is wrong.

"How wrong? Is it more than fifty grand or less?"

"I've told you – I can't tell you."

Whatever the amount, it will not cover the hundreds of hours that Sharan and her husband have invested her case over the years, to say nothing of the wear and tear and the heartache.

Saturday, 27 April. Newsroom, Centre Desk. Tithers posts a note in Newsroom Log about the Sharan Sandhu case.

'We have nearly 300 staff and 24 hours of output … Last time I looked at the stats, the majority of our staff are women; 17% are from ethnic "minorities", as UK counting would have it; 12% have been recruited from the BBC's services in foreign languages. Amongst the people working for World Service News and Current Affairs we have staff who are German, Ghanaian, Romanian, Nepalese, Brazilian, Serbian, Colombian, Australian, American, Greek, Chinese, Bulgarian, Finnish, South African, Indian, Albanian, Russian, Portuguese, French, Cuban, Uzbek, Sri Lankan, Vietnamese, Burmese, Angolan, Swedish …'

The reaction in Talkback further reflects the authentic range of our diversity.

- 'It sounds exactly like a list of exotic animals at a zoo.'
- 'Alas, New Zealand and Ireland have been cruelly omitted from the list.'
- 'So were the Quebecois.'
- 'And what about Yorkshire with our mixed Brigantean, Anglo-Saxon and Norse heritage?'

I ask Newsinf* to send me a selection of Sharan Sandhu stories from the past week's newspapers.

'Colonial Club Blocked My Progress At BBC' (*Evening Standard*); 'Boozy White Males Keep Empire Alive At World Service' (*Daily Telegraph*); 'Tribunal Told Of BBC's

Colonialism Mentality' (*Independent);* 'World Service "Boys Club" Ruled Over Ethnic Staff, Tribunal Told' (*Scotsman*); 'BBC Accused Of Colonial Clique ' (*Times*); 'Colonial Outlook At World Service' (*Guardian*). 'Newsgirl: My Beeb Race Hell' (*Sun*).

Monday, 29 April. Newsroom, Centre Desk. The acting Editor sent across from Telly Centre to cover for Mary Hockaday's maternity leave is a man called Bill Rogers, one of Steve Mitchell's most trusted lieutenants. Bill is affable and he's a proper news operator. He is just the sort of person we were hoping might become our next Editor, except for the fact that he's a virtual stranger to World Service and understandably is feeling rather bewildered by the multi-ethnic, multi-cultural variousness lurking round every corner of every corridor in Bush House. World Service is full of people accustomed to thinking of Britain as a foreign country which is one reason why it doesn't feel like anywhere else in the BBC. The only big, open-plan space inside Bush House is the Newsroom. Everyone else works in cubby holes divided from each other by the thin wooden walls and frosted glass panels that represented the acme of office design, circa 1939. Bill summons me down to the Third Floor for an honest conversation about the Sharan Sandhu case.

He says one of the things taken into account by the BBC team that decided to settle her case was the nature of the evidence that was still to come. He says they particularly did not want any evidence coming out about the historic 'vomit session' of WSNCA Band 10s that precipitated the installation of John Morrison as Editor.

The 'vomit session' was an Awayday of WSNCA Band 10 editors convened at Telly Centre in May 1999 with a senior Human Resources executive present and an independent therapist/facilitator asking the questions, most of them framed to liberate our pent up frustrations with 'the deterioration of morale and industrial relations' in the department. Opinions were solicited on how best to 'restore the health of the organisation'. Among the problems identified were 'bullying' and 'personal abuse' with particular reference to female staff. The two people present at the vomit session who later agreed to give evidence for the BBC against Sharan Sandhu at her tribunal hearing would therefore have found themselves in a very questionable position.

"The thought of the vomit session getting into the public domain," says Bill, "made the team very uncomfortable indeed. The very phrase 'vomit session' would have given the press a field day."

He says I must be very naïve to think I could have presented evidence about the vomit session and not risk harming the BBC's reputation. Who, he asks, did I think was going to play my role when Hollywood got around to making its account of the Sharan Sandhu affair – Harrison Ford?

Another of my career-limiting impulsions finds voice.

"Sharan was overlooked and de-motivated. She was denigrated behind her back. A whole succession of managers ignored her case. Sharan's bosses always had more important things to worry about than being fair to Sharan Sandhu."

I certainly had been prepared to talk about the vomit session.

"In that case," says Bill, "I'm glad we made the right decision."

CHAPTER THREE

The Expenses Scandal

Wednesday, 22 May. Royal College of Surgeons, Lincolns Inn Fields, London WC2. Newsroom Band 10 Awayday. Tithers has booked us into the airless room at the back of the building used for storing broken chairs. The clock on the wall is stuck at a permanent 3.44. The agenda is as follows:

1. Illustrated bulletins: They're a mess, what are we going to do?
2. Guest slot: Sonia Magris and Kevin Marsh will be explaining how Radio News is getting into shape financially for the move to New Broadcasting House in 2007.
3. Morale: how to raise it after the alleged damage inflicted by the Sharan Sandhu case.

Illustrated bulletins. Tithers outlines the problem. All of the Newsroom's straight-read bulletins used to start at the top of the hour, with headlines. The Harding-style illustrated bulletins that have replaced them start at one minute *past* the hour, after a programme billboard*. Our friends in Current Affairs love this idea because it puts news inside a Current Affairs programme instead of in front of it.

Unfortunately, everyone knows that no listener, anywhere, has ever tuned in late to the World Service in order to miss the news and go straight into a Current Affairs programme. News comes first like night follows day, i.e. always and forever. Even more unfortunately, in the glad rush to replace straight-read bulletins with illustrated bulletins, the leadership forgot to make provision for the fact that there are several hours, out of the 24 in every day, when WSNCA doesn't have a Current Affairs programme on air. What happens then? Now that all the news bulletins on our warm and accessible English network start at one minute past the hour there are one-minute 'gaps' all over the schedule – at exactly those times when listeners are tuning in for a news bulletin.

And there's another problem. These gaps at the top of the hour are owned by another department – World Service Presentation not by WSNCA. The folk in Presentation have improvised a one-minute package to fill the gap but it is a stop-gap and it sounds like one.

"You're listening to the BBC World Service. It's 12 hours Greenwich Mean Time. The time in Lagos is 13 hours; in Tokyo it's 21 hours; in Rio de Janeiro it's 9 o'clock. The headlines: A president has made a speech; a bus/plane/train has crashed; scientists somewhere have discovered an important new discovery ... (fade up newsy muzak) ... Now, here with that news in detail, is Joe Blah ..."

We look at each other in silence. Does any other radio station in the world begin its news bulletins by reminding listeners of the time in Lagos? Does it sound cool? Or does it sound like a stop-gap cobbled together by someone not thinking straight after tripping over a loose shoelace? We argue together for an hour to no definite conclusion and decide in the end to do what we usually do. We set up a committee and call it a working group.

Guest slot. Sonia Magris and Kevin Marsh hand round a document called *World Service Money* which confirms that WSNCA's annual budget is £18 million, 70 per cent of which goes on staff wages. They then hand round a document called *Digital Plus* which predicts painful efficiency savings for BBC Radio News ahead of the move to New Broadcasting House in five years' time. After lunch, Sonia and Kevin go back to Telly Centre and those of us who are still awake wonder aloud if it might be a good idea to go home early. Tithers insists on moving on to item 3.

Morale. To counter the alleged bad effect of the Sharan Sandhu case Mary & Co. want us to come up with ideas to raise our collective profile and get some good press. We grumble into our tea and biscuits. Morale in the Newsroom is always low. That's how we like it. We are rota fodder. Only managers have names, the rest of us are known by our initials on the rota board. In return, we get a day off for every day on and we dearly love those days off. That's why, when we need to raise morale, we like to go home early.

⊱──⊰

Thursday, 23 May. Newsroom, Centre Desk. I am sitting with my feet on it, reading *Ariel* * as part of my job.

> 'The measured tone and unflappable manner of the news presenter all too often masks a backstage drama. Television News will never be for the faint-hearted. But nor should its high pressure environment be an excuse for bullying or

intimidation. To this end, *News 24* morning editor Simon Waldman – a BBC newsroom veteran – has drawn up a code of behaviour to help promote courtesy and civility.

'"It's all part of the 'Making it Happen' pledge to value people," explains Waldman. "We want TV News to be a nicer place to work …" He dubs the pilot scheme, which may be extended throughout BBC News, "The Polite Police" …'

I worked with Simon briefly on the *Six O'Clock News,* when Richard Sambrook, now Greg Dyke's Director of News, was cutting his teeth as a shift editor in the Telly Centre newsroom. As I recall, most of us were reasonably polite to each other most of the time although the presenters could be a bit waspish. If a Polite Police force is now seen as the way forward for BBC News we're done for.

›•–◦–•‹

Friday, 24 May. Newsroom, Centre Desk. I am starting to wonder how much longer it's going to be before someone shows Greg Dyke one of his yellow cards, followed by a red.

'The BBC is facing criticism,' says the *Evening Standard,* 'after Greg Dyke ordered hundreds of workers to wear silly hats and play hoopla during a team building seminar. Over 400 workers from across Britain took part in the £250,000 event at a conference centre as part of the director-general's drive to improve creativity. Activities included a pep talk given to a group by Mr Dyke, while others kicked footballs into goals

and played fairground games … The gathering of managers
was part of the biggest meeting of top personnel since the [sic]
Mr Dyke's "cut the crap, make it happen" initiative ...'

My own yellow card lies in the SDE's drawer*, along with the key
to the stationery cupboard, the Newsroom's collection of orphaned
spectacles and the 'Emergency Procedures' folder containing the
instructions to be followed in the event of the Queen's sudden demise.
They were funny, Greg's yellow cards, when they first arrived on
Centre Desk. They made us laugh for about ten minutes. Then we
got on with the news and forgot about them. Despite Mark Byford's
loyal exhortations, Greg Dyke's 'Make it Happen' campaign has
utterly failed to capture the imagination of Bush House. It looks to us
like tawdry self-publicity. As Bill Rogers is slowly discovering, we
think of the rest of the BBC as a foreign country of which we know
little and care less.

Tuesday, 25 June. Fair Selection Course, BBC Training Centre,
Marylebone High Street, W1. I am here because Bill Rogers has
decided that although I cannot be punished by electric shock for my
part in the Sharan Sandhu case he can sentence me to a course of
compulsory re-education. No one who has not been on the BBC's
Fair Selection course is allowed to sit on recruitment or promotion
boards. By sending me here our acting Editor is signalling that after
years of wriggling out of my Band 10 responsibilities I am at last
being lined up to sit on a selection or a promotion board.

The whole idea of the Fair Selection policy is to armour the BBC against equality at work legislation. For example, it is deemed unfair to ask a candidate's colleagues how they rate him or her in the job because that might allow subjective judgements into the selection process. Fair Selection is intended to eliminate subjective judgements. Candidates must be assessed only on their performance at an appropriately constituted selection board. Which explains why WSNCA employs so many people who can waffle about Current Affairs at selection boards but can't write a news story when they're plonked down in front of a computer screen with a deadline looming. Selection in favour of the competent and reliable is what we need not more promotions for those who are simply keen to get on.

━━◦◦━━

Tuesday, 2 July. Newsroom, Centre Desk. Good news for lovers of prestigious, over-priced glass and steel office blocks with knobs on. Greg Dyke's plans for New Broadcasting House have been given the go-ahead by Westminster City Council. Initial estimates put the cost of the project at some £400 million. The architects have done as they were told and shaved something off the height of the proposed building and incorporated more stone into its façade. Various senior bosses have been stamping around the *Ariel* office, trumpeting superlatives.

'Landmark piece of architecture ...' 'A project of real conviction ...' 'An adventure to be shared with the people ...'

The re-vamped artist's impressions of New BH make it look exactly as one might expect an eight-storey glass box to look when bolted on to an older, more elegant structure.

'Trashy and glassy …' 'Portentous not stylish …' 'Incongruous and probably not half big enough …'

The Magris/Marsh presentation about the budget for BBC Radio News sounded an alarm and I heard it. There is going to be a nightmare of a squeeze when the time comes to fit the whole of World Service News and the whole of Telly News and all of Radio News *and* BBC Online into one enormous Newsroom in New BH. The only way it can be achieved is by getting rid of people through job cuts because that's the only way our bosses know how to 'save' money. In five years' time the Band 10 editors of my generation will be regarded as deader-than-dead wood and we know what will happen then. No way will our bosses be able to deliver New BH on budget, on schedule and fit for purpose without job cuts, if at all.

>-+◦-O-◦+-<

Tuesday, 9 July. Newsroom, Centre Desk. I phone the BBC expenses people at their Cardiff HQ to find out what's happened to the claim I submitted in January after paying with my own money for David Blow's retirement lunch. They give me a much clearer idea of what to do to get my £280 back: start all over again. Unfortunately, the person in charge of the Newsroom's expenses forms has run out of expenses forms. Nor can she print off a new batch of forms because her computer isn't working. I cannot print an expenses form from my own computer because it isn't fitted with the right software. I decide to leave things for a day or two until I cool down.

＞＜＞-○-＜＞-＜

FROM: Alan Le Breton, Managing Editor.
SENT: Wednesday, July 10, 2002.
SUBJECT: Greg Dyke video address.

'To accompany this month's 2-way brief, we've been sent a short video presented by Greg Dyke, mainly about 'Making it Happen' ... I'd like to be sure you can make it available for your groups ... Give me some feedback during the normal feedback process. And don't forget the 'event' on Thursday evening ...'

＞＜＞-○-＜＞-＜

FROM: Richard Sambrook-Private.
SENT: Wednesday, July 10, 2002.
SUBJECT: Event –Thursday, 11 July.

'Reminder. BBC News Event.

Sports & Games: Dodgems, Football, Tennis, Volleyball, Softball.
Food: Barbeque, Wok Bar, Candy Floss & Ice Cream.
Drink: several bars – including a Pimms Bar.
Dancing: DJ Emma B and Disco.
No need to RSVP but bring your BBC i.d.'

＞＜＞-○-＜＞-＜

FROM: Chris Moore-BU.
SENT: Thursday, 11 July.
TO: Richard Sambrook-Private

'Unfortunately, Richard, I am working tonight. Our bulletins at Bush House go out every hour of the day, every day of the year. But thanks for the invitation'

FROM: Richard Sambrook-Private.
SENT: 11 July 2002.
TO: Chris Moore-BU.

'Indeed Chris – it's always a problem to find the right time because so much of what we do (including News 24, World, Radio 5 Live, Newsgathering and Online as well as Bush) requires 24 hour 7 days a week working. However I hope you'll be able to come to a future event. Best Wishes, Richard.'

Tuesday, 16 July. BBC Training Centre, Marylebone High Street, London W1. My course of compulsory re-education continues. Today's indoctrination is called 'Leading a Team in News'. Eleven of us have gathered in a back room with a facilitator who goes round the table asking us to say who we are and what we hope to get from the course.

"My name is Chris Moore. I joined the BBC in 1979, since when I have had four Directors-General shot from under me. I am currently a Band 10 Senior Duty Editor in the Newsroom at the World Service. I think this is the fourth time I've been sent on a BBC leadership course. The message clearly isn't getting through."

Wednesday, 17 July. BBC Training Centre, Marylebone High Street, London W1. Day Two of 'Leading a Team in News'. A cuff-linked *apparatchik* from a BBC outpost called 'New Media' addresses us on the subject of leadership. He says it has a moral dimension. Any boss who tells lies cannot be an effective leader. He then tells us that Greg Dyke is a charismatic, cut-the-crap kind of guy who is an indisputably good thing when compared to John Birt, "although, er, let's be fair to John, he wasn't always the, er, robot he was made out to be. He did push through some very necessary reforms."

After lunch we divide into teams for a team-building exercise involving balloons, pieces of string and an egg. My team's egg gets smashed first go. Later, we have to fill in a Self Perception Inventory. I emerge with high scores as both a Shaper ('highly motivated ... a great need for achievement') and a Team Worker ('perceptive and diplomatic ... generally popular'). In the discussion that follows I learn that I am also regarded by my fellow course members as a bit of a Grump, ('disengaged ... hostile to change ... a moaner.')

Wednesday, 17 July. Newsroom, Centre Desk. I phone the BBC Expenses Unit in Cardiff. The problem, they explain, is how to frame an expenses claim without a proper receipt. All the documentary evidence of my expenditure on the David Blow retirement lunch has been lost along with my previous claim. The solution is to send Cardiff a letter of explanation, signed by my line manager and counter-signed by the chief financial officer of my Division i.e. BBC News.

It sounds deceptively simple. If my claim was for £2.80 instead of £280 I would file it under H for Hopeless and forget the whole thing. But £280 is about the size of my overdraft at the end of every month and the M.O.T. is due on the car. Since January, I have been subsidising the BBC by running an overdraft to pay for David Blow's retirement lunch, which I'm guessing is more than Greg Dyke (salary last year, including benefits, £469,000) has ever done for a much-respected former BBC Vienna correspondent.

Thursday, 18 July. Haverstock Hill, London NW3. Haverstock Hill is where I come to work on my relationships. I used to be able to cycle the full distance from SW4, arriving short of breath and damp with sweat. Today, for the first time, I arrive straight from work, nice and fresh.

"I am so angry."

A man in my position – 46 years old, married, two children, two cats – must be in some kind of trouble when he finds himself ranting about his bosses while paying someone a pound a minute to hear about it.

"Really, *really* angry ..."

Alan is my psychotherapist. He is bearded, be-spectacled and very controlled in his movements. He follows certain protocols. For example, he always uses the same stiff-armed greeting to beckon me in when he opens the door. He always waits for me to lie on the couch before seating himself. Usually, as soon as I lie on the couch I dry up, lie silent, wrestle inwardly with my demons. This time it's different.

"The lunatics have taken over the asylum ..."

The last thing I did before leaving the Newsroom was check my e-mails. One of them was from the Chairman of the Board of Governors, Gavyn Davies, thanking me for my role in the BBC's magnificent year of achievement. No mention of the 1.8 per cent pay rise that Greg Dyke has decided to impose on us while paying himself and his top 18 managers more than £5 million pounds in salaries, bonuses and benefits.

"They are ripping off the BBC and getting away with it ..."

By the age of 46 most proper adults have given up on righteous indignation. Isn't it normal in publicly funded, hierarchically organised bureaucracies for those in charge to run things for their own benefit? I tell Alan about my latest experience of a BBC leadership course.

"Right at the end, our facilitator drew a diagram on her flip chart to show the three typical ways in which bosses relate to their workers. One type is the nurturing, supportive parent: 'Here, let me help with that. I'll do it for you a couple of times until you get the hang of it...' On the other side is the critical, authoritarian parent: 'Pull your socks up! You should have got the hang of it by now! If you don't try harder, there'll be trouble ...' The third option is not based on the parent-child model but on equality and respect, adult to adult. 'No way,' I said. 'Adult to adult is just not my style.' "

Sunday, 21 July. Newsroom, Centre Desk. At last, someone serious has put into words what BBC staff are thinking right now about Gavyn Davies and Greg Dyke and their cronies. Thank you, Martin Bell. Thank you, *The Independent on Sunday*.

'At a time when out-of-control capitalism is increasingly discredited for its dodgy balance sheets, unearned incentives and golden handshakes for under-performing executives, the BBC throws more than £1 million [in bonuses] at its senior managers to bribe them to stay at their posts. They are public service broadcasters. They are already well paid ... Let us take the example of Mark Byford whom I know of old. He is now director of the BBC World Service, but once he was a down-table sub on the home news desk assigning reporters to cover floods and court cases ... On top of a salary of £211,000, he neither needs nor deserves his bonus of £69,000 or benefits of £14,000 ... The BBC is not a business. It is a public service.'

Tuesday, 23 July. Newsroom, Centre Desk. First night shift. Greg Dyke's video nasty awaits. It was recorded at that Awayday in Docklands that was full of clowns and hoop-la. Greg appears in one of his signature shiny suits and no tie. We gather round the telly in Tithers' corner office to look and learn.

"When I launched 'Make it Happen'," says Greg, "I said we would find a way of making everyone in the BBC a part of it …"

In close up, on bad quality video, his vocal rasp perfectly matches his physical features. Greg Dyke looks and talks like a top geezer whose vocation is selling dodgy Taiwanese hair dryers from the back of a van in a Walthamstow car park. No way does Greg radiate charisma as he barks platitudes at his captive audience. It's hard to decide: is he channelling an emperor without clothes or some demented North Korean demagogue? Us whingers and moaners stand defence-less in the face of 'Make it Happen'. Arise, Sir Greg.

><+>-0-<+>-<

Monday, 29 July. Newsroom, Centre Desk. Breaking news on Greg's *Palace of Varieties*. The *Telegraph* carries an article about New Broadcasting House, complete with computer-generated graphics. The Newsroom inside New BH will be an enormous bear-pit taking up the whole basement, with four mighty columns to keep the upper eight upper floors from crashing down. Anyone who knows the first thing about corporate architecture knows there's no room for dead wood in such an exciting spatial environment. Centre Desk may be bored of my doomsday predictions but that's not going to stop me predicting – no one will be prepared to defend us when the battle for space turns into a battle for survival.

><+>-0-<+>-<

Sunday, 11 August. Newsroom, Centre Desk. The dumbing down of the World Service continues apace with user-friendliness oozing from every broadcast portal. Our new top-of-the-hour headlines glow with the fake warmth of a plastic log fire in the lobby of an out-of-season Turkish hotel.

"With world news every hour, this is the BBC ... (newsy muzak) ... It's 2 o'clock in Hong Kong, 10 o'clock in Dubai and 9 o'clock in Nairobi. And wherever you are, you're very welcome to join us here at the BBC World Service ... (more newzak) ... Hello. I'm Joe Blah and at 6 o'clock GMT these are the latest BBC news headlines (... blah ... blah ...) Details of all those stories next, here on the BBC World Service, and remember – you can get the latest world news from us at any time on the internet, at BBC News dot com."

First the illustrated bulletins, now the global time-checks with muzak. '*Welcome to join us?*' No, no, no, dot com. Rage, rage against the dying of the light.

FROM: Chris Moore-BU.
SENT: 12 August 2002.
TO: Compass Catering.
SUBJECT: Canteen not getting any better.

'Yesterday, Sunday 11, at 0730 hours, there was green mould on the bread in the canteen but no coffee and no eggs. Later, when I went back for a cup of tea, the milk came out of its carton in a solid lump. Thanks for a great start to the day.'

Monday, 19 August. Management Suite, Third Floor, South East Wing, Bush House. Once more unto the breach over David Blow's expenses. I tell WSNCA's finance person what I have been told by the expenses unit at Cardiff. I explain about the letter I have to write and the signatures and the counter signatures. He says he will deal with it. He says Sonia Magris is coming over. He will give my letter to her and she will take back to Telly Centre to get the endorsement of News Division's Chief Finance Officer. I write my letter and hand it over with no great hopes. At least I've given it my best shot.

<hr>

Tuesday, 27 August. Newsroom, Centre Desk. Happy days are here again. The clouds above are clear again.

'Well, I'm back,' writes our newly returned Editor in the Newsroom Log, 'and actually happy to be so … (so far anyway!) … It's good to see everyone again and get back to the real world. Over the next week or so I'm going to catch up with as many people as possible, and find out what's what … Or you can catch me in my new home in the corner office on the 3rd floor. And once I've done that, I'll let you all know my thoughts about where WSNCA goes from here, and what we need to work on in the months ahead. Mary (Hockaday).'

<hr>

DATE: Wednesday, 18 September.

FROM: Cardiff Expenses Unit, S1005, Ty Oldfield.

TO: Christopher Moore.

'Remittance No: 2000907524. Remittance Amount: 283.50 Sterling.

… Funds will be in your bank account three working days after the date of this advice …'

Unbelievable. Astounding. Thank you. Thank you. Things don't always end badly. Sometimes they just take a lot longer than you originally thought.

CHAPTER FOUR

Libel Awareness

Sunday, 6 October. Newsroom, Centre Desk. Night shift. At about 2230 hours the AFP news wire pops up with an 'urgent' saying that a major offensive has been launched by the Ivory Coast government against rebels in the northern city of Bouake. I ask the overnight writer known to the rota as LAM to start writing a snap in anticipation that a second source will soon confirm the story. I tell him not to use the phrase 'major offensive' but to talk about 'fighting' or 'clashes' since AFP is probably only talking about two truck-loads of guys firing shots into the dark.

The chat between LAM and myself is overheard on the News-gathering* Intake desk. Without waiting to be asked, the new Intake assistant gets on the phone to our correspondent in Ivory Coast, Paul Welsh. She thinks she is being pro-active, which is good. But if she had asked me first I would have told her not to wake up a correspondent in the middle of the night for what might well turn out to be a storm in a piss pot. When Welsh expresses derision about the reliability of AFP's sources in Bouake the Intake assistant relays his warning, with added high-pitched decibels.

"Paul says to be very careful. You aren't snapping it, are you? Not with only one source?"

I tell her that AFP's source is its own correspondent in Bouake.

"Paul says AFP don't have a correspondent in Bouake."

"They do now."

I tell LAM to carry on writing his snap. The Intake assistant calls across.

"Paul says to be very cautious about the line about a major offensive," she shrills. "He says AFP call it a major offensive every time there's any kind of shooting."

By the time LAM's snap is written the Associated Press is also reporting a 'major offensive' at Bouake so I green it and announce on the Newsroom tannoy that the latest fighting in Ivory Coast is going into the headlines at midnight, at number two. I ask SMJ to turn the snap into a story for the top of the hour. By the time it's ready for greening Reuters has also come up with a snap about Bouake. But while all three international news wires are talking about a 'major offensive' our story merely refers to 'fighting'.

At about five minutes to midnight, the News Traffic tannoy announces that Welsh is filing: government forces in Ivory Coast are attacking rebels near Bouake. I realise too late that he is dictating news copy not filing a generic minute* - BBC News jargon for a short, sharp audio burst from a correspondent of 60 seconds or less that can be turned around quickly and broadcast immediately. I ask the Intake desk to make sure that Paul files a generic minute as well as his news copy and go over to warn the *World Briefing* desk to make a space for it in their midnight running order*.

Back at Centre Desk I find that Welsh has rung off without filing a generic minute. This is not the procedure. The Head of Radio News, Stephen Mitchell, has made it clear that the generic minute, not news copy, is the priority for all correspondents. I ask the Intake assistant why Welsh did not file a generic minute. She said she asked him for news copy.

"Twenty minutes ago," I explain instructively, "when the story was on AFP only, that was the time to ask for news copy – when we needed confirmation of the event. Not now. We now know what's going on – fighting. What we need now is coverage."

The Intake assistant says sorry. She says she thought we needed news copy.

"The story had already been written by the time Welsh came up. Ivory Coast was our second headline. We didn't need copy, we needed was something to put on air ..."

"Please don't ..." says the Intake assistant running from her desk in tears.

I turn to the Intake editor. He looks at me. I show him the palms of my hands.

"What did I say?"

"She thought she was doing the right thing, Chris."

I blame Fair Selection. It is not sufficient to select and promote people who perform with confident enthusiasm at selection boards. We also need nous, knowledge, savvy, common sense, an awareness of the trade. Nous comes from learning on the job from those with experience to share. Without our World Service craft skills we're no better than the rest, and that's not good enough.

⊢━◆━○━◆━┥

Friday, 11 October. Telly Centre. Various editors from across BBC News have been brought together in a windowless conference room for a libel seminar. The embarrassment of the Oryx case has made refresher courses in the law of defamation compulsory. One of the legal eagles in attendance is Glen del Medico. The last time I saw him was in Journalist Training, *circa* 1980, when he gave us a talk on libel and explained why we ought to call it defamation. Glen's thick black hair is now snow white.

Richard Sambrook arrives, the master of locking the stable door after the horse has bolted. He talks about the need for everyone in BBC News to "update our libel awareness" without mentioning the word Oryx. There has been no public word on how much the settlement is going to cost. One rumour says the damage to the BBC News budget will mean job cuts.

On the way home I pop in to Broadcasting House for lunch. Greg Dyke is in the canteen, mixing with his workforce like a proper geezer should. He is sharing a table with three middle-aged men who seem to be agreeing with every word he says and laughing uproariously at his jokes. He takes his pudding with him when he leaves – a banana and a tub of yoghurt. *Geezer*!!

Tuesday, 15 October. Newsroom, Centre Desk. BBC Television News numbers a few sloppy writers among its correspondents and a popular Centre Desk hobby (when I'm on shift) is to collect examples of their telly-centric crassness. One of their guys covering the aftermath of the bomb explosion in Bali that killed more than 200 people has chosen to record his piece-to-camera* in front of a stack of empty coffins.

"These coffins are on standby," he intones. "Pain feels the same in any language …"

———o——

Tuesday, 22 October. WSNCA Management suite, Third Floor, South East Wing. I am supposed to be on leave today but I've had to come in to Bush House to work on the short-listing of candidates for the Broadcast Journalist (Band 7) selection board. I'll be sitting on the panel with someone from Human Resources and a Current Affairs editor. There are more than 260 forms to sift through. My eyeballs start to hurt after half an hour. The shortlist drawn up by my Third Floor colleague ends up twice as long as mine so either he has been too lenient or I have been too strict. We finally agree on a shortlist of sixty candidates. *Sixty*! Then he tells me that the Human Resources chaperone assigned to us has negotiated a work-life balance whereby she only works parent-friendly hours, 1000–1630, no exceptions. That means our 60 interviews will have to be spread over *three weeks!* I think if Bill Rogers had offered me the choice between electric shock therapy and three weeks cooped up with Human Resources and Current Affairs I would have taken the volts.

———o——

FROM: Paul Waters.
SENT: 23 October 2002.
TO: Chris Moore.
SUBJECT: Things That Are Difficult to Say.

'Things that are difficult to say when you're drunk: innovative; preliminary; cinnamon. Things that are very difficult to say when you're drunk: specificity; unwritten British constitution; transubstantiate. Things that are impossible to say when you're drunk: thanks but I don't want to sleep with you; no I don't fancy a Chinese meal; Oh, I just couldn't – no-one wants to hear me sing.'

FROM: Mary Hockaday.
SENT: 31 October 2002.
TO: Band 10s.
SUBJECT: Richard Sambrook's letter:

'You'll have seen Richard Sambrook's letter about possible redundancies across the News Division. I'd like to make it clear that this does not mean WSNCA is having to reduce numbers in any drastic way. We have had to offer possible efficiencies to WS for next year, but I am so far pretty confident that these would not impact much on staff numbers …'

FROM: Internal Communications.
SENT: 07 November 2002.
SUBJECT: Today's *Guardian* article about BBC Finances.

'This is being sent to everyone in the BBC.

This morning's *Guardian* article is inaccurate … There is no BBC crisis and there is no financial black hole in News … Discussions are going on about how we will meet our savings targets in the next financial year … We will seek to avoid compulsory redundancies but, of course, we cannot give guarantees … Mark Damazer, Deputy Director BBC News.'

Monday, 23 November. Home desk, London SW4. I dreamt I was at a BBC careers seminar. The venue was some sort of school dining hall with child-sized tables and plastic chairs. The folk on my table sent me to queue at the hatch for the dinners. By the time it was my turn the food had almost run out. The man serving was from my own table. He put my tray to one side while he dealt with the person behind me, thereby leading me to understanding that I was going to get some of the choice cuts that he had been saving up for us. After waiting for some time he handed me back my tray loaded with the same slop as everyone else.

Monday, 11 November. WSNCA Management suite, Third Floor, South East Wing. BJ7 selection boards. Our first candidate is a former-Soviet person with a PhD. in International Relations. She left Moscow University the same year I graduated, worked for state television and then went to America on a study programme which turned into a sort of career. Her application form is full of academic qualifications and impressive sounding scholarships but she doesn't have a clue what kind of job she might be applying for and, fatally, she is unable to name a single programme broadcast by the BBC World Service. Eight previously agreed questions form the basis of our interview, with a maximum of two marks for each answer.

"What did you give her?" I ask when the interview is over and our first candidate has closed the door behind her.

"Nought," says Human Resources.

"Yes, nought," says Current Affairs. "How about you?"

"Nought."

The three of us have given Dr Clever-but-Dimovich nought for every answer she gave. We check our score-sheets. Out of a possible maximum score of 48 she has scored precisely *nul points*. Current Affairs and Human Resources cannot believe it. They've both seen some bad interviews in their time but this one has been uniquely bad.

"Well at least we were consistent."

"Yep. No arguments there."

"What the ..?"

Five minutes later we are still shaking our heads incredulously and saying *fnarr fnarr* when the Editor's secretary sticks her head around the door to see if we're ready for the next candidate. Only 59 more to go.

━━◦━━

Friday, 22 November. Newsroom, Centre Desk. There is a tradition in the Newsroom of not making news out of the BBC unless it is absolutely necessary. I have never seen eye-to-eye with this policy because it seems to me that anyone who listens regularly to the news on the BBC can be assumed to have an interest in the affairs of BBC News, especially when it has made the news itself, for all the wrong reasons.

CEN 2100 BBC LIBEL

The BBC is to pay £500,000 in damages to a diamond company which it wrongly linked to Osama Bin Laden and al-Qaeda. The company – Oryx Natural Resources – sued for libel after a BBC domestic television channel (BBC1) broadcast the report in the aftermath of the September-the-eleventh attacks. Correspondents say the BBC will also have to pay legal costs of around £300,000.

Monday, 2 December. Newsroom, Centre Desk. At the back of the Newsroom, through the soundproof door that leads to studio S46, is a short corridor leading nowhere – the locker room. Every wall and desk in the Newsroom has been moved or altered since I've been working here but the locker room has always been the locker room. Today, all the lockers have been forced open to allow a grand re-distribution of locker keys, many of which have been lost or lent out so that no one now knows exactly which locker belongs to whom.

My own long-lost locker, when I open it, contains a folding umbrella which I am quite glad to see again and a packet of crisps two years past its sell-by date. I taste one and spit it out straight away. I also find a big stack of stale Newsroom test papers in there, from the days when every candidate for a job in the Newsroom had to pass the Newsroom Test. How proud I was, as a newly-promoted Band 9, to be given the responsibility of administrating those tests; how old I feel unearthing their mummified remains.

I can find no record of how anyone in Mary & Co. might have performed in the Newsroom Test, if any of them ever sat it, but several once-famous names are represented, including one colleague who left in a blaze of glory after having a novel accepted for publication, which is my own preferred exit plan. This person scored ten-and-a-half out of 25 on the news quiz, giving the occupation of Enrique Cardoso as 'opera singer' instead of President of Brazil and naming Belarusse [sic] as the capital of Estonia, having first crossed out Belgrade. The candidate wrote pretty well, though, and was given a job despite thinking the Dutch team, Ajax, were the reigning champions of the English football league.

⊶•○•⊷

Saturday, 20 December. Newsroom, Centre Desk. The BBC World Service was 70 years old yesterday. There was a special phone-in to mark the event, presented live from the top of Table Mountain in Cape Town, South Africa. Mark Byford fielded listeners' questions from around the world in a live phone-in. When one irritated listener asked him why he had switched off the short-wave transmitters to North America and Australasia he replied that the money saved by switching off the transmitters had been needed to fund audibility in Afghanistan. If I remember correctly, the reason given at the time for the switch-off was to save money for investing in re-broadcasting on FM stations around the world. Only afterwards did Al-Qaeda attack New York and Washington, leading to the American attack on Afghanistan, which persuaded the Foreign Office to demand an increase in BBC broadcasting to that country. So the correct way to think of Mark's reply, as anyone will confirm who's been on a libel refresher course with Glen del Medico, is that it reflects an entirely appropriate diversion of BBC resources to where they're needed rather than a convenient blurring of the facts.

CHAPTER FIVE

Shock and Awe

Sunday, 5 January 2003. Newsroom, Centre Desk. The new year begins where the old one left off, with Greg Dyke under fire.

'BBC's news palace in peril,' says *The Observer.*

A rich property company is seeking an injunction to block work on New Broadcasting House on the grounds that the BBC is breaking an undertaking made in the 1920s not to build above a certain height.

'Being forced to scrap its plans for Broadcasting House would be a disaster for the BBC.'

⊢◁●◁─○─▷●▷⊣

Friday, 17 January. Bush House, working lunch, Room G22, North East Wing. Two platters of bottom-of-the-range sandwiches lie on the table, curling at the edges under the blast of the air-conditioning. Steve Mitchell and his good mate Bill Rogers have come over to talk to us about BBC Values. Greg Dyke has decided we need some new ones. Every member of staff will be getting a letter about it.

"I was going to start by apologising for the temperature in here," says shivering Steve, "but it should be you who's apologising to me."

He says he was sceptical about 'Make it Happen' when it was first introduced a year ago but now – ahem – he's been "won round". We re-arrange our arms across our chests. On the wall of G22 hangs an oil portrait of Cecil Lewis, who fought in the same squadron of the Royal Flying Corps as Albert Ball VC. Lewis shot down eight Huns over the Western Front and survived. After the Great War of 1914 – 1918 he was recruited by fellow subaltern, John Reith, to be a pioneering radio producer at the BBC. When that stopped being fun he went to Hollywood to write scripts and seduce film stars. I am fairly sure that neither Bill nor Steve will be seducing Halle Berry or writing for Steven Spielberg any time soon, nor winning the Military Cross for gallantry. *Ariel* combat is more their style.

▸•▸•○•◂•◂

FROM: Stephen Mitchell.
SENT: 24 January.
TO: Radio News.
SUBJECT: Efficiencies in News.

'Dear Colleague, As you know, Richard Sambrook wrote to everyone in News a while ago setting out the need to make efficiencies in the 2003/4 budget … Within Radio News, there should be no compulsory redundancies. We're closing or have closed 21 posts – out of a total of 68. Six are currently unfilled, 12 are contract jobs or attachments … and at the time of writing we have three agreed redundancies … '

▸•▸•○•◂•◂

Sunday, 2 February. Newsroom, Centre Desk. Night shift. Empathy is not normally expected in our professional handling of world events but sometimes we have to report something that leaves us feeling saddened and diminished. Tonight, as part of our sequence about the crash of the American space shuttle, *Columbia*, we want to testify to the human spirit of its doomed astronauts.

CEN 0300 SHUTTLE FINAL MINUTES

The *Columbia* was twenty-one minutes away from landing when mission controllers (in Houston, Texas) noticed a sudden loss in temperature readings in the hydraulic system in the left wing. Shortly afterwards, signals ceased from the temperature sensors elsewhere. NASA engineers sent a signal to the crew, then asked them to repeat a muffled radio message. After a period of silence, the *Columbia* commander, Rick Husband, began to acknowledge messages but he was cut short after just two words. There was a burst of static and then no more. Mission Control's radio calls met only silence. By that stage, the space shuttle *Columbia* was a white trail of wreckage streaking to Earth.

The journalist who wrote that is identified on the Newsroom rota by the initials SMJ. None of our listeners will ever know his name but they all know his work when it touches them.

▸┄◂┄◦┄▸┄◂

Saturday, 8 February. Newsroom, Centre Desk. It has taken me all this time to get around to reading last week's *Sunday Telegraph Review* with an article in it by Rod Liddle in which he describes his exit as the Editor of Radio 4's *Today* programme.

'A sort of adolescent spasm took hold and I thought, in the end, this: how could I live with myself if I agreed to the terms and continued as editor? I just couldn't do it. It was, finally, the impetuous decision of a 15-year-old boy.'

A lot of BBC journalists feel like that these days. A clown is running the circus. Our bosses are guzzling at the trough. No wonder we succumb to the occasional career-limiting spasm.

<hr/>

Monday, 17 February. Newsroom, Centre Desk. I am reading-in* at the start of the early shift when the phone rings on the Intake desk. It is the Secretary General of NATO, George Robertson. I hear the Intake editor say something about getting the senior editor on duty. I pretend to hide under my desk.

"Tell him I'm on holiday."

The Secretary General of NATO wants to complain about the headline on the lead story of the World Service news bulletin he's just heard. I call up our current Top on Intake's screen.

'NATO has resolved the bitter dispute among its members over American preparations for a war against Iraq. The alliance has agreed on measures to protect Turkey in the event of a conflict.'

"The first thing that's wrong," says Mr. Robertson, "is that there never was a dispute about any 'American preparations for a war'. The disagreement all along was about reinforcing Turkey, and that's what we've settled. Secondly, the reinforcing of Turkey is to take place now, immediately, not in the event of anything. I've been hearing it wrong every time I listen to the BBC."

I point out loyally that the offending headline was written by the night shift and suggest that the bulletin will improve dramatically now that they have gone home to bed.

"We must have got hundreds of stories wrong about NATO over the years," I say. "How come you're only phoning us now?"

"I suppose I just couldn't restrain myself."

I apologise on behalf of the World Service for spoiling his breakfast and get an extra quote out of him by asking how the Americans are reacting to news of the deal, which gives SMJ a nice new line to work into the story in time for the top of the hour.

<hr />

Tuesday, 18 February. Newsroom, Centre Desk. Someone in the BBC has sent us all a glossy brochure telling us what to think.

'BBC Television – a chance to make up your own mind.'

The letter inside pretends to be from Greg Dyke himself.

'Dear Christopher, I'm sure you'll agree that it's frustrating when the BBC is accused of 'dumbing down' and of failing to produce distinctive and diverse television programmes ... The brochure

I've included with this letter is being sent to journalists, MPs and other opinion formers to demonstrate the rich and varied television output we broadcast during 2002 … I'm sending the brochure to you and all other members of staff so that you can use it as ammunition to argue against those who criticise us … Yours, [signed in a thick, backward sloping hand] Greg.'

One of these days, one of these actual, real-life Centre Desk days, I am going to tell Greg what I really think and click 'send'.

'Dear Greg … Fanks for the brochure, yeah, but I am returning it coz I gave up telly yonks ago, when you started dumbing down all the programmes on it, know what I mean? Regards to Sue your partner as ever, arf, arf, [signed in green ink with a right-leaning wobble] *Radio Rental Goes Mental.'*

▻⦁⧁⦁◅

Wednesday, 12 March. Broadcasting House, Portland Place, London W1. I pop in for lunch and to inspect the renovations. The building's front portal is boarded up. Eric Gill's iconic statue of Ariel is shrouded in protective plastic. A giant hole in the ground is taking shape where Egton House used to stand, the former home of Radio One.

Up in the eighth floor canteen of Broadcasting House, gazing north, I meditate upon the transience of all things. Beyond the roof-tops of Portland Place and Regents Park lies Langdon Park Road where I used to live in a shared house in the days when I had breakfast here every morning before heading down to report for duty at Journalist

Training on the third floor with a styrofoam cup of coffee in my hand. Nostalgia is one of the things I will miss most when the old BH canteen closes for good. I'm starting to miss it already.

Saturday, 15 March. Newsroom, Centre Desk. Each 24-hour day is divided on our rota between three separate teams of journalists, the early shift, the late shift and 'Dawns', as night shifts are known. 'Doing Dawns' is manageable because there tends to be less news overnight and there are no bosses around. Late shifts are the easiest because the late team doesn't take over full responsibility for the bulletin until 1700 hours and it hands it over to 'the Dawns' at 2130. Early shifts are the most stressful because a) they start at 0730 hours which means getting out of bed ridiculously early to get to Centre Desk on time; b) most of the world's news happens on the early shift so there are lots of decisions to call; c) the bosses are around all day long wanting to be taken seriously; and d) we arrive sometimes to find that the bulletin left over by the Dawn shift is so old it's in a coma.

CEN 0700 IRAQ DIPLOMACY

Iraq has submitted to United Nations weapons inspectors a report they've been demanding on chemical weapons agents. It's meant to explain how and where Iraq disposed of its stocks of VX nerve gas 12 years ago. A second report, setting out what became of its stockpile of anthrax, has been promised. The Americans say the submission has come too late. President Bush and his two main allies – the prime ministers of Britain and Spain, Tony Blair and Jose Maria Aznar – are to hold an emergency summit on Sunday in the Azores.

The White House says the meeting will aim to bring the diplomatic process at the UN to a conclusion.

The newest element here seems to be the American rejection of the Iraqi report so I ask SMJ to freshen the story by putting the line about 'the submission has come too late' on top. This standard Centre Desk procedure is known as re-nosing* the story. With 20 minutes to go before the 0900 bulletin goes on air the editor of *World Briefing* wanders over to say he can't find any audio anywhere of any American rejecting the Iraqi report as having come too late. Nor is 'the submission has come too late' line contained in any BBC correspondent's despatch.

"And there's no 'rejection' line," says SMJ, "in Reuters, AP or AFP."

How could the night shift have got the lead story so wrong? The editor of *World Briefing* suggests they might, in their tiredness, have confused Washington's rejection of a Chilean resolution at the UN Security Council with the Iraqi report on nerve gas. Whatever the explanation, 'Operation Re-Nose' has turned to ashes in our hands. The whole basis of our inherited lead story is in doubt.

"Bloody hell."

"You can say that again."

"Where's the used tape?"

Once a story is written on Centre Desk the procedure is for the source material used in its construction to be stapled together and put in the used tape box for the benefit of anyone needing to check the facts. Of course, when we look in the used tape box the source material for CEN 0700 IRAQ DIPLOMACY is nowhere to be found.

And the clock is ticking. There is a single straw to clutch at – the Azores emergency summit between Blair, Bush and Aznar.

"It's still eight hours away," says SMJ. "That's a hell of a long trail."

We like to report things that have just happened or events that are happening right now. Looking ahead to something we expect to happen is known as a trail, fake news. But with ten minutes to airtime what choice is there?

SMJ starts turning our lead story into a trail of the Azores meeting while someone else puts a KILL slug on the 0700 IRAQ DIPLOMACY story to make sure that it's dropped immediately from all outlets. At times like this I hate being reminded that Bush House is a massive human beehive full of radio services broadcasting Centre Desk's news 24 hours a day on the assumption that it's usually right. It is the worst possible time for the Newsroom cleaner to arrive with her industrial-sized vacuum machine. She is heading for Centre Desk like a Force-10 dust storm.

"Fuck!" says SMJ all of a sudden. "My story's *gone*!"

He is staring at a blank computer screen. ENPS has swallowed his story and is refusing to spit it out. None of us has ever seen this before. With six minutes to go we have no lead story and no headlines. All we have is a blank screen and a howling vacuum cleaner. Apart from that, the only thing I can hear is a dull throbbing in my ears.

"Don't worry," says SMJ. "I think I can remember the gist of it."

He re-boots and starts again. We have entered the zone known in the trade as a nightmare scenario. Meanwhile, the cleaning woman is bumping her machine round to our side of the desk to give us the benefit of her jet-stream at full blast. I try to focus only on what is in front of my face – draft headlines. Headlines to what, exactly? What is the news? I have no idea. There *is* no news, just a howling vortex with the word 'Azores' trapped meaninglessly inside it. Someone taps me on the shoulder from behind.

"Chris, can I just ask if you've …"

In five minutes, millions of people – including the bosses of my bosses - will be tuning in to the World Service to get the news and unless we can think of something RIGHT NOW all they'll hear is the vague hissing sound of … zilch. And someone has chosen this very moment to tap me on the shoulder.

"No," I snarl without looking up. "Please. Not now. Don't ask. I am *very busy*."

It is LG, possibly the only person in the Newsroom at this time of the morning who's worked here longer than I have, first as a typist (in the days of typewriters) now as a BA, a Broadcast Assistant. We are old friends. We have never had a cross word in more than 20 years.

"Sorry, Chris," she says in a hurt voice. "I just wanted the key to the stationery cupboard, that's all."

⊶─◦─⊷

Sunday, 16 March. Home Desk, London SW4. George W. Bush's long-awaited war in Iraq is almost upon us. Spring has arrived, the daffodils are in bloom. Fat, pink magnolia buds unfurl in the expensive front gardens of Kennington. I cycle to work with the after-taste of an unpleasant dream in my head. I was on a ledge, high above a sheer fall. It was the Sigiriya rock fortress in Sri Lanka, re-located to an English moorland. Women and children strolled below my perilous perch, licking their weekend ice creams. There were smooth hand and foot holds in the rock but no sure way down. Even now, having worked my shift and returned home, I can still feel the powerful after-vibe of high anxiety.

Saturday, 22 March. Newsroom, Centre Desk. It is only Day Three of the invasion of Iraq and already the war is going badly on the Dawn shift. The fragile coalition between Newsroom and Current Affairs is fraying under the strain of rolling thunder*. When the Newsroom's bulletin producer goes down to the Current Affairs studio (S36) with his scripts, the programme producer won't give up his chair to let him sit at the control panel. Our guy has to stand behind the studio manager* with the result that he has nowhere to lay his scripts. So he calls the wrong cue*. Which means that the wrong audio is played. Which makes us sound bad. Which means I have to go down to the Third Floor yet again and make like I've been on a training course about people management. It's not a good way to start a war.

Sunday, 23 March. Newsroom, Centre, Desk. The Dawn shift is settling into its war routine. It starts with air raids on Baghdad, followed by news briefings in Washington, followed by fruitless attempts to find out what the Turks are up to in northern Iraq, if anything. Then there is a lull from about 0200 to 0500 when, with break of day in Iraq, our correspondents embedded with American and British forces start calling in on their satellite phones. This morning, at about 0600 hours, Adam Mynott, our embedded correspondent in the southern Iraqi town of Umm Qasr, gets caught up in a battle while the pooled camera feed* is beaming out live pictures. It is the best bit of live reporting I think I have ever seen on telly. By the time we're getting ready to leave Bush House at 0730 the whole world is watching.

Of course, the incoming early shift is completely underwhelmed. At one point during the shift handover* the Newsroom reporter wanders over with a question.

"What's another word for Division?"

"What do you mean?"

"You know, the American 101st Division. What's another word for that?"

"There is no other word for it. That's what it's called."

"So I can't call it a Brigade, or something?"

"No. A Division is a Division."

There are quite a few young journalists in World Service News and Current Affairs who can tell you interesting stuff about the Brazilian economy or minority rights in Bulgaria but not much about warfare. They have no model in their heads of how armies are organised (Divisions composed of Brigades; Brigades of Battalions; etcetera.) or why the war in Iraq is taking the shape it is. They don't understand what armies have to do in order to win battles. This failure to mediate intelligently between the event and the listener – the essence of radio journalism – will be glossed over in the weeks ahead. The script has already been written. The leadership has decided that the World Service is going to have a very successful war.

Saturday, 29 March. Newsroom, Centre Desk. My favourite sound-bite of the war so far comes from the crew of a British armoured vehicle in Basra trying to get an infantry squad to do the right thing.

"Fucking wait! We've got to get those fuckers out of that fucking house first."

Sunday, 30 March. Newsroom, Centre Desk. News comes in that an old friend has died while covering the war. I feel physically sick. Gaby Rado is dead. He 'fell' off a hotel roof in Suleymaniyah. Gaby and I used to sit next to each other in the Newsroom at Telly Centre when I was there doing my on-the-job training and he arrived from Radio Leicester. We both disliked the Telly Centre regime equally, except that Gaby's burning ambition was to get on screen and mine was not, which meant he had to hold his tongue when his bright ideas were slapped down. When he moved to Channel Four News I thought it was exactly the right place for him. And now he's gone.

Monday, 31 March. Newsroom, Centre Desk. My favourite news despatch of the war so far has been translated for us by the Arabic section.

CUE: Spring in Baghdad is marked by the short-lived flowering of heavily scented citrus blossoms and roses. Baghdad is not a city of high-rises and most Baghdadis live in villas not apartments and have their own gardens. The gardens usually have taps which dispense what is called 'may khabut' or water not suitable for drinking. The BBC's Arabic Service interviewed their correspondent's gardener, Muhammed, and asked him if he had been working since the bombing.

TAPE: I've stopped work since the bombing started. Usually I would work in private gardens, cutting the grass, clearing weeds round the bushes, weeding the grass, watering, planting. I was doing between six and seven gardens a day. Q: Is there any water shortage? A: No, there's both drinking and non-drinking water available. Q: What kind of flowers do you like? A: I like gerbera, gardenias, gazanias (kind of daisy in bright colours, brick reds and yellows), kalanchoe (a succulent plant with roundish leaves and bright red or orange flowers). At the moment everything is in season. What's just started blooming now is the citrus blossom – orange, lemon, mandarin. They are out now on the trees. My favourite is 'razqi' (jasmine), gerberas and roses. They smell so beautiful. Q: Have you got a garden? A: In my house … in my house, no. (Pause) Unfortunately. Q: You said you'd stopped work since the war started, why is that? A: Whenever I go to my customers' houses, I find they're not there. Gone to check on their relatives after the bombing or gone to work.'

⊢•⊷○•⊷•⊣

Friday, 4 April. Home Desk, SW4. A fan letter arrives direct through the letter box rather than arriving *via* my editor at Little, Brown.

'Dear Mr Moore, I've just read your excellent book, *Continental Drifter,* and found parts of it hilarious. I think I possess a similar sense of humour to your own. Thanks – a truly great read. I wonder if you could help me since we are going on a tour of Belgium later this year …'

Wrong writer. Wrong book. Wrong everything. This is the third time my publisher, Little, Brown, has sent me one of Tim Moore's fan letters since I stopped getting any of my own for *Trench Fever*.

▷━◆━○━◆━◁

Tuesday, 8 April. Newsroom, Centre Desk. Favourite viral e-mail of the war so far.

SUBJECT: 'Why did the chicken cross the road?'

Saeed Al-Sahaf, Iraqi Minister for Information: "The chicken did not cross the road. This is a complete fabrication. We do not have a chicken. There is no road. The Americans will be defeated and their bones will lie scattered in the desert."

George W. Bush, President of the United States: "It doesn't matter why the chicken crossed the road. What matters is, whose side is he on? There is no middle ground. Freedom will prevail. God bless America."

Tony Blair, British Prime Minister: "I agree."

Dr Seuss, children's author: "Did the chicken cross the road? Did he cross it with a toad? Yes, the chicken crossed the road. But why he did, I've not been told."

Martin Luther King, civil rights campaigner: "I envision a world where all chickens, whatever their colour or creed, will be empowered to cross any road to fulfil the highest calling of which they are capable."

Bill Gates, richest man in the world: "e-Chicken 2003 will not only cross roads but will file your important documents and balance your chequebook."

Albert Einstein, theorist: "Did the chicken cross the road, or did the road pass beneath it?"

Bill Clinton, former American President: "What is your definition of 'cross'?"

Colonel Sanders, chicken fryer: "Did I miss one?"

⊢━◦━⊣

Wednesday, 9 April. Newsroom, Centre Desk. The battle for Baghdad appears to be over. Our correspondent, Andrew Gilligan, is announced by News Traffic just before I am due to depart for the 0900 Bush House editorial meeting. Gilligan says his Information Ministry minders have not shown up for work so he is able to report freely for the first time in weeks. The implosion of the Iraqi regime predicted by George Bush and Tony Blair has happened. I duck into the 0900 editorial meeting, drop the Gilligan bombshell and leave.

Minute by minute, for the rest of the day, Centre Desk steers World Service through the military occupation of Baghdad. Anyone listening to us, at any point during the day, gets the whole picture. We establish the hard military facts, such as can be verified by our reporters on the ground; we have the atmosphere from the streets; we have reaction from around the world. Does our Editor congratulate the Newsroom? She does not. Only after all the editorial calls have been made, live, in real time, in rapid succession, one after the other, relentlessly, does she make contact through a top line message on ENPS.

'Chris, now that we've had our fun and seen the Saddam Hussein statue toppled over isn't it time to go back to the real story?'

I am at a loss to know how to reply. Our fun? The real story? What can she mean? The humanitarian relief effort? The arm-less, scalded babies? The mayhem and confusion in the Kurdish north?

She has her qualities, our Editor, but handling the people in her Newsroom with sympathy and understanding after a hectic battle is not one of them. I stare at my screen. I feel deflated, drained and weary. Hardly anyone has escaped from Centre Desk all day, even for ten minutes. Every one of us knows that the toppling of Saddam's giant statue in Firdaus Square is the defining moment of the war so far. First we watched the Iraqis put a noose round Saddam's statue and saw their rope break. Then we watched American military engineers move in with a steel hawser to do the job properly. That precise moment, when the armoured might of the American military brought down the hollow figure of Saddam Hussein, tells the world all it needs need to know about the kind of war we're dealing with.

When I show the Editor's message to SMJ he shakes his head in disbelief. All that is left is to crank out my last headlines of the day and pack up the empty sandwich box.

CEN 1630 TOP

Three weeks after their invasion of Iraq, American-led forces have taken up new positions in the heart of Baghdad and now occupy key sites on both sides of Tigris river. As American tanks swept through the city, crowds came onto the streets to denounce Saddam Hussein and to attack the symbols of his power. In one central square a towering statue of the Iraqi leader was toppled to the ground. In Washington, President Bush said he was heartened by developments. The British Prime Minister, Tony Blair, warned that the wider war was not yet over. Arab states say they now want to see Iraq run by Iraqis.

CHAPTER SIX

The Body Fluid Response Team

FROM: Richard Sambrook – Internal.

SENT: 15 April 2003.

SUBJECT: Big Conversation.

'This email is being sent to all staff in BBC News.

As you will have seen from Greg's email of 27 March we are planning a BBC-wide communication of the Making it Happen change plan on 15 May, 10.30–12.30pm. This is entitled the Big Conversation and it will include a series of divisional events, team briefing meetings and some pan-BBC events … I know how busy everyone is, but *please* do everything you can to make time for this event … I'd like as many people as possible from News to watch the May 15 film and take part in the discussion … Regards, Richard.'

><

Monday, 28 April. Home Desk, London SW4. My wife shows me a Christian magazine with a big photo of Mark Thompson on the cover. He is now head of Channel Four Television but when I first worked with him he was careering upwards at Telly Centre as editor of the *Nine O'Clock News*.

'... In my view, the public service broadcasting created by John Reith ... was a reaction to the loss of religious faith ... The BBC was founded pretty much overtly with that idea ... Broadcasting at least can be the glue that holds society together ... When I was Controller of BBC2, I did a programme called *Seeing Salvation* with Neil MacGreggor (which was mounted simultaneously as an exhibition at the National Gallery). Now that was a brilliant religious series as well as a great art series. We just need to bring some flair to it ...'

The reason no one remembers *Seeing Salvation* (apart from me, one episode) is because it was a pious yawn from beginning to end. If Mark Thompson is serious about replacing Greg Dyke as Director-General of the BBC at some future date, which I assume he must be, I would strongly advise him not to mention *Seeing Salvation* on his application form. And I would also suggest urgent action re. the beard. There will be at least one talented, energetic, high-powered woman on the shortlist and he won't want to look like a badly shaved cat's arse by comparison.

⊶━◦━⊷

Friday, 16 May. Newsroom, Centre Desk. It can feel slightly disorientating to re-enter Bush House to start the first day shift after the 12-day absence caused by four days off, four Dawns, then four more days off. It can feel, as someone once put it, a bit lowering. I can never suppress the hope, when I leave for home at the end of my fourth day on, that the things that are broken will have been fixed by the time I return. I should have learned by now. No one fixes the air conditioning or the computer glitches or the vending machine, which has recently developed the nasty habit of spewing hot chocolate on my shoes instead of black coffee. No one finds time to sit down next to newly arrived colleagues with the earnest desire to give them the on-the-job training they need. We bodge and bumble from one shift to the next like a gang of shonky builders hurrying to get to the next job before finishing the one they're on. There's no time for routine maintenance on Greg Dyke's mad carousel, no pause for thought. Thankfully, trawling through my inbox, I realise I have missed the latest set-piece extravaganza which Greg was so eager to impose on us all.

<hr />

FROM: Greg Dyke.

SENT: 12 May 2003.

SUBJECT: The Big Conversation.

'Three days to go! Have you made arrangements to join us for the Big Conversation … It will affect every single one of us who works here, so please make every effort …I've asked managers to make every effort to spare you for that time … We are announcing big, bold changes … And don't forget, everyone who takes part will get the chance to win tickets to the FA Cup Final and Wimbledon … Greg.'

When I express relief that I managed to miss the whole of 'The Big

Conversation' because I was on Dawns someone tells me that out of the 1000 staff employed at World Service only about 20 turned up. The National Union of Journalists, NUJ, organised a boycott in Bush House as part of its protest against the summary dismissal of two translators in the Arabic Service. Little stickers have appeared around the building showing Greg Dyke in the guise of 'Comical Ali', the derided Iraqi Information Minister, Mohammed al-Shahaf.

'BBC VALUES: INSTANT DISMISSAL.
NUJ BOYCOTT COMICAL GREG MAY 15.'

No one knows how much Comical Greg is spending on 'Make it Happen' but none of our bosses is making a fuss so he'll get away with it. Mark Byford will have to back down over these two translators, though. According to the NUJ, the BBC has broken the law in the way it's sacked them. So they'll get the pay-off they want and the taxpayer will pick up the tab.

<hr />

Sunday, 18 May. Newsroom, Centre Desk. I do wish our correspondents would check what their despatches are going to sound like before filing them through News Traffic.

"The head of the UN Children's fund, Carol Bellamy, says a surge in acute diarrhoea is hitting Iraqi children ..."

Writers aiming for the ear rather than the eye should read their words aloud, and listen, before hitting us with stuff.

Tuesday, 10 June. Newsroom, Centre Desk. The newspapers are not letting go. The drip feed of leaks to the *Daily Mail* just keeps on leaking.

'BBC Chairman Gavyn Davies makes regular day trips to the Cote d'Azur by private jet to play a round of golf. Costs are estimated at £20,000 based on average charter fees of £5000 an hour … Mr. Davies, who has been dubbed commander-in-chief of Tony Blair's cronies, works three days a week for the BBC. The former banker is thought to be worth £137 million … After his round Mr Davies, whose wife Sue Nye is political secretary to Chancellor Gordon Brown, has lunch at the club's gourmet restaurant before heading home to his £2 million house in South London.'

Thursday, 3 July. Newsroom. It is eerily quiet when I arrive at 1130 to start my late shift. Very, very quite. No phones are ringing. No one is complaining peevishly about how freezing cold it is because of the air conditioning. The temple of the news gods just doesn't feel right. BR is sitting in the SDE's chair on Centre Desk.

"Chris!" he says. "What are you doing here?"

"What do you mean?"

"Shouldn't you be at the Awayday?"

"What Awayday?"

"You forgot about Steve's Awayday?"

Tithers is having an Awayday? The one that was originally scheduled for 25 June which then got cancelled?

"That Awayday."

Guffaws, jeers and sniggers ripple out from Centre Desk to the Newsroom's regional desks and beyond. Hilarious! Chris has come in to work a shift instead of going to Tithers' Awayday with Mark Byford.

"Are you winding me up? Mark Byford?"

BR is working an attachment as Tithers' temporary deputy. If Mark Byford is at the Awayday, why isn't BR there?

"Well," he says, "we brought in VM as a stand-in SDE but she went sick as soon as she got here so I've had to stand in for the stand-in. I'm going along at lunchtime. Let's go together, then it won't look so bad."

The venue is an elegant room at the Royal Society of Arts in The Strand, a ten minute walk away. BR and I get there just in time to hear Mark Byford's thoughts on the way ahead for World Service. He sprawls under the chandelier like a Medici cardinal in his throne. By draping his jacket over the back of one chair and his tie over the back of another he has managed to occupy his entire side of the conference table.

"I were just saying, Chris lad, that what you guys do, you guys in the Newsroom, it's absolutely central to the whole World Service ethos. It flipping well is. News is the absolute foundation of everything we do …"

I hate myself for not asking, if we are the absolute foundation, why it's taken him four-and-a-half years to get around to meeting us in person.

" … News is the engine for change in World Service ... We depend on you totally … No relationship is perfect … United we stand, divided fall …Any questions?"

"Mark," I say, "when we are moved to New Broadcasting House you'll be bringing together BBC Television News, BBC Radio News, World Service News Programmes, BBC World, BBC Online, News 24, and more than 40 language sections. Who will be in charge – the people at Telly Centre or us lot from Bush House? Realistically, Mark, how many in this room do you think you'll be taking to New Broadcasting House?"

"Very good question … That's just the kind of conversation we need to be having right now … The move to B.H. is a huge project … We need a strong idea about the sort of adjacencies we're envisaging …"

>−•≫−◦−≪•−<

FROM: Bill Rogers.
SENT: 14 July 2003.
TO: Chris Moore-BU.
SUBJECT: Leadership.

'Dear Chris, We're nominating you for one of the new BBC leadership courses based at Ashridge, in the category 'established leader'. The basic time commitment is an initial two days at Ashridge (near Berkhamsted) 27 and 28 October 2003, and a final two days on 27 and 28 May 2004. In between is a three-day workshop (venue tbc). You can express a preference between 10/11/12 December and 17/18/19 December … Please let me know which would be better ...'

Ashridge is a stately pile that's been converted into a business school specialising in corporate clients facing culture change. Greg Dyke has block-booked huge chunks of time there so that hundreds of middle managers from across the BBC can be put through their paces. The idea is for us all to be infused with renewed energy and commitment to 'Making it Happen' in the BBC. God knows how much it's going to cost in licence fees but probably millions.

FROM: Mary Hockaday.
SENT: 17 July 2003.
TO: Band 10s.
SUBJECT: A few things.

'I've been horribly absent from communications meetings this week … but there's something I want to tell you about. I've been asked to join the Ashridge Leadership Development programme on attachment as a tutor for six months from September. It's something I'm very interested in and it's bound to be a fascinating experience. It does however feel a terrible and very short-notice wrench, and there's important work to be done later this year about the shape of things in the future ...'

"What? She's only been back six months and now she's off again?"

Since being made Editor, Mary has been away from her desk almost as often as she's been at it. We know what that means. Someone is grooming her for higher things. Which means she probably won't be with us very much longer. Is it my imagination or is our Tithers walking around with a new gleam in his eye? Someone has to watch the mice while the cat's away, especially if she's being groomed for higher things and therefore likely to create a vacancy for a promotion in the not-too-distant future.

┝╺◆╸◯╺◆╸┥

Tuesday, 22 July. Newsroom, Centre Desk. Night shift. The rota is going through one of its periodic mental breakdowns with the result that all kinds of folk are turning up on my team whom I haven't seen for ages. One of them is PIV who's been drafted in as a writer. We always like finding PIV's initials on the rota because a) he's reliable and b) he's got a handsome new guide dog called Laddie who, like his predecessor, exerts a calming influence on all the sighted humans who come within his radius. I am typing away in the wee small hours when Laddie comes round on patrol. He nudges me a couple of times with his nose.

"What do you want, Laddie, eh? What do you want, eh?"

Nothing apparently. He licks his chops and disappears. A few seconds later I become aware of a bad taste.

"Ugh!"

I swivel in my chair to see if anyone else is in trouble and nearly put my foot in a heap of khaki-coloured dog doo. A couple of folk wander over from *World Briefing* holding their noses.

"What's going on?"

Laddie's going on. He's squeezing out a second instalment.

"He must be sick or something!"

No matter how hard PIV tries to enforce a strict regime on Laddie's intake, some of us (not me) can't seem to restrain the urge to spoil him with surreptitious titbits – stray scraps of chicken tikka masala, for example, left congealing on a canteen tray over on the South Asia editor's desk. At once, like a finely calibrated leadership machine, my hard-earned leadership skills kick in.

"Cover it up with the waste paper bin."

"We'll need a skip for that lot," says ANC.

A couple of Current Affairs folk come up from the Third Floor to marvel for themselves. And then security arrives.

"Thank God you're here."

The security guy pulls a horrified face and calls up someone on his walkie-talkie. In a couple of minutes two men arrive from Facilities Management with a mop and a bucket and an orange plastic suitcase labelled 'Body Fluid Response.' Within minutes, the problem has been dealt with and the soothing, restorative scent of garden herbs, squirted from an aerosol can, is wafting over Centre Desk. Which is fine until the same men return to replace the well-Laddied carpet tiles with new ones of a colour that doesn't quite match.

"Sheesh!" sniffs ANC. "That carpet glue smells worse than the shite."

><+--0--+-<

Wednesday, 23 July. Broadcasting House, W1. I pop in for lunch on my way home from Haverstock Hill. In my bachelor days I used to eat in the BBC's various canteens a lot, rambling around London at odd hours of the day and night. They offered good, cheap meals for shift workers until John Birt decided that the people who worked shifts for the BBC weren't worth a generously subsidised canteen, no matter how many of them had to work anti-social hours to produce BBC programmes and keep them on air.

I choose a table from where I can check on the progress of the redevelopment while re-energising on a plate of sausage and mash. As well as the hole where Egton House used to stand there's a now a huge gash down one side of the old BH building, exposing its innards. I can see right into the corridors. The fire extinguishers are still on the walls. So are the notice boards, with their notices flapping. Cartoon-sized workmen load debris into a skip and when it's full a crane hoists it up and sets it down a 100 feet below. Up empty, down full. Up, down. Up, down.

It is like watching Breughel's *Tower of Babel* being un-built, stone by stone. The steel frame of Broadcasting House is emerging like a mighty skeleton being picked clean. It was constructed in concentric layers around an inner core of concrete studios. This hard inner core is being steadily exposed as the builders make room for the structure that will arise. It so obviously provides a metaphor for the work I'm doing with Alan on Haverstock Hill that I start to snigger and inadvertently snort custard up my nose.

⊢-◆-○-◆-⊣

Thursday, 14 August. Newsroom, Centre Desk. Night shift. In summer when the dawn arrives early in our hemisphere it's hard to stay focused on the news; I want to pack my bags and go. Chained invisibly to our desks, bored with the dribbles of news coming through on ENPS, we flick channels on the telly from one breakfast show to the next. The generic chirpiness is inescapable. This morning the BBC is making a big deal of the nation's A-level results. Some school, somewhere, has agreed to accommodate the requirements of BBC News by bringing some spotty kids in early to open their brown envelopes.

"Hold on … ," I say.

There's something familiar about that school hall. As the camera pulls back for a wide shot, my suspicions are confirmed.

"Hey! That's where I sat my A-levels. Right there. In that assembly hall. That's my old school. On telly!!"

I don't know why I should be so excited but I leave the Newsroom after the shift handover with almost a spring in my step. I hated that school but it made me feel good to see part of my life validated, howsoever tangentially, on the telly. Whatever our news, it is always real life to someone; in this case me.

⊱─◦─⊰

Wednesday, 20 August. Newsroom, Centre Desk. Log Advisory.

'Last night at 2230 (August 13) Helen Clark rang the Band 10s' phone in the *World Today* office to do an interview. She was put on hold and left there for quite some time (her assistant said 20 minutes but I presume this was an angry exaggeration). It is only after a morning of apologising to two of her press people that she will talk to us again. Helen Clark, for those of you who might need to be reminded, is the PRIME MINISTER of

New Zealand. She regularly appears on the BBC, not just the World Service. Even if whoever answered the phone didn't know who she was, they should have done what you should do with all calls – find out who it is on the line and what their business is. It's called journalism.'

CHAPTER SEVEN

Lord Hutton Inquires

Thursday, 21 August. Bush House car park. Having stacked my bike in the bike racks I am strolling across to Centre Block to get a cappuccino from the Arcade café when Mark Byford's official car sweeps into its reserved parking space. It is one of those big, van-shaped people-movers and it is daubed all over with 'Make it Happen' buzz words and catch-phrases. And here he is, springing out right in front of me!

"Chris, mate! How are ya?"

I indicate my cycle helmet and pannier.

"A bit sticky today, Mark. I could do with one of those air-conditioned chariots you've got."

"Ha ha. Where do ya ride in from?"

"Clapham."

He pats his belly.

"That'll be doing ya some good then?"

I pat mine.

"Not at my age."

"Ha ha."

"Ha ha."

I hate myself. Fraternising with the boss. Me. Fraternising.

▷─▷─○─◁─◁

Tuesday, 2 September. Law Society Hall, Chancery Lane. WSNCA Awayday. The Law Society's breakfast pastries and croissants used to be memorably light and crisp but today they're limp and stodgy imitations. Perhaps they're a harbinger of the budget cuts heading our way. The warm-up act features two Current Affairs editors who have put together a PowerPoint presentation about the World Service audience and the message is we're in trouble. Having lost nearly all of our European listeners since the collapse of communism, South Asia is going the same way. Our audiences in Hindi, Urdu and Bengali used to be numbered in the tens of millions but these days they're all watching telly. And it's the same in the Middle East. The invasion of Iraq has lost the BBC the trust of many Muslim listeners. Even in Indonesia and Somalia they're now apt to regard the World Service as the lying mouthpiece of an infidel invader.

"So what kind of an audience *do* we have?"

"Basically, the only listeners we can be sure of are those who can't be bothered to change their habits or those who don't have a choice. In other words, old people and Africans."

Which bring us neatly to a discussion of next year's budget. Out of a total expenditure of some £19 million we are being asked to save £465,000 in the year 2004.

"So over to you," says the Editor. "Any bright ideas?"

It is too early in the Awayday for bright ideas. Besides, we're Band 10 journalists not SPS managers. It would be great, once in a while, if someone in Greg Dyke's BBC could actually model leadership instead of paying themselves bonuses for merely talking about it.

"If no one is listening to us in English in South Asia any more,"

I ask, "why are we investing in one editor, two presenters and three producers for a South Asia edition of the *World Today?* That's a big chunk of output wasted, if no one is listening."

I am expecting nervous laughter and the usual frigid blast of disapproval from the top end of the table. I am well known, whenever the subject of BBC nastiness is in prospect, for trying to divert attention towards the Third Floor. That's because, although I fully understand the need for *some* Currents Affairs, it gobbles up far too much money in proportion to the understanding it delivers of world events - money that could be better spent preserving what Mark Byford calls our absolute foundation, the news. On the other hand, we do need something to keep the transmitters warm between bulletins. This time, instead of regarding me with exasperation the Editor seems positively relieved.

"Thank you, Chris. That's obviously a radical solution but it's probably the kind of big idea the department needs to be thinking, given the amount of money we have to save."

The person the Editor has put in charge of Current Affairs instead of herself is called Liliane Landor. She is usually a feisty mother hen when it comes to protecting her Third Floor brood. Liliane says that scrapping *The World Today* for South Asia would certainly be bad for morale – really, *really* bad – but leaves it at that. No fireworks.

That's when it dawns on us. The idea of scrapping the South Asia edition of *The World Today* is already under discussion by Mary & Co. Everyone around the table suddenly realises that they can't think of a single good thing to say about *The World Today* for South Asia. Especially when they remember that the programme's most respected champion, Andy Whitehead, is off in America for six months on a freebie scholarship thing.

The World Today was conceived as a breakfast programme for the whole world, in English, starting at 2230 hours in East Asia and ending in Europe at 0730. Maybe it seemed like a good idea back in nineteen-ninety-something but times have changed. All round the table people are waking up to the fact that *The World Today* now sounds like a busted flush. I think we all know what's going to happen over the next few months to the one editor, two presenters and three producers of *The World Today* for South Asia. Andy Whitehead is in for a big surprise.

Friday, 5 September. Newsroom, Centre Desk. Log Advisory.

'See you in six months … I'm off on holiday tomorrow and then when I get back to join the Ashridge leadership programme … I shall miss you all … Bill Rogers will be looking after things from next week, and I shall keep in touch. Good luck, Mary [Hockaday].'

Sunday, 7 September. Newsroom, Centre Desk. Last of four night shifts. I go down to the Third Floor with the intention of raising the morale of the team putting out *The World Today*. The overnight Band 10 says he doesn't know what I am talking about.

"Oh, didn't Liliane tell you? They're scrapping the *The World Today* for South Asia. Mary says we've got to save half a million quid and instead of saving it by taking slices of budget from here and there, she's going to take it in one big hit. And since the Hindus, Pakistanis and Bangladeshis have stopped listening to the *The World Today* the South Asia edition looks like being the big hit. I thought Liliane would have told you by now."

"What?"

The Third Floor's South Asia shift editor has butted in. Scrapping *The World Today* for South Asia? No way! What did Liliane say?

"She said she could see that scrapping *The World Today* for South Asia would be bad for morale but -"

" 'Bad for *morale*' ?"

"Well, it's only an idea. Liliane wasn't outraged or anything. She just looked a bit … weary."

"And Mary liked the idea?"

"No. She just said it was the kind of big idea we needed to be talking about. Sorry, guys. I thought you knew. This all happened last week."

⊷•⊶

Sunday, 14 September. Bush House car park, 2130 hours. The limousine lurking outside South East Wing is Greg Dyke's Lexus. His chauffeur sits in the back seat watching telly. Greg is giving evidence tomorrow at the Hutton Inquiry into the death of David Kelly, a Ministry of Defence official who killed himself after being named as the source of a BBC story about the government exaggerating the case for war against Iraq. Bush House is the closest BBC building to the Royal Courts of Justice in the Strand, which is where Lord Hutton is based. The BBC team in charge of presenting the BBC's evidence has been meeting regularly in the management suite of World Service News and Current Affairs for the past couple of weeks.

~~~

Monday, 15 September. Bush House, Centre Block. I have barely sat down on Centre Desk with a cup of afternoon tea from the canteen when one of our correspondents arrives, looking like he's just seen a car crash. He's come straight from the Hutton Inquiry where Greg Dyke has been giving evidence; he needs to unburden himself before collecting his thoughts to write his despatch.

"We just sat there looking at each other in complete amazement," he says of his fellow scribes. "That man is a total buffoon. He can't use words. He literally could not explain what he meant. If that testimony had been televised Greg Dyke would be the laughing stock of the nation. He sat there like some sort of oaf. I don't think he actually finished any of his sentences. Lord Hutton looked embarrassed."

~~~

Wednesday, 17 September. Haverstock Hill in reverse – Oxfam bookshop first, then Broadcasting House for lunch, then Haverstock Hill. The dismantling of the old BH seems to have hardly progressed since my last visit but that's because it is being taken apart piece by individual piece. A human chain of demolition men fills a skip by passing lengths of old ducting from hand to hand. Down below, in the immense excavation next to All Saints Church, steel beams have been installed to stop the sides caving in. I tell Alan I have not been able to choose a date to quit therapy. I haven't even looked at my diary.

"That probably means you're not ready to finish any time soon."

"What about cutting down to one session a month? Would that be feasible?"

"When we finish our work together," says Alan, "we will finish for good. The ending is a big part of therapy. You will be ready for it. We will have talked it through. You will not go until you are ready."

┣┅┉┅◇┅┉┅┫

Sunday, 21 September. Newsroom, Centre Desk. There's a note from the acting Editor in Log Advisory.

'A film crew from *Panorama* will be in and around my/Mary's office, on Saturday, shooting scenes for a Hutton special. Bill Rogers.'

┣┅┉┅◇┅┉┅┫

Monday, 22 September. Bush House car park. Greg Dyke's Lexus is back. Up in the Newsroom, a masseuse is wandering around with a clipboard, booking sessions for stressed out news hacks suffering from the habitual bad posture of folk who spend their four days on hunched over a computer keyboard in Bush House and their four days off hunched over a keyboard at home. I book myself in for a 20-minute neck and shoulders massage but by the time 1430 comes around I am knee deep in Ivory Coast and have forgotten all about it until someone reminds me.

"I'm too busy. Stuff it."

"You'll still have to pay."

"Nobody said anything about paying. I thought it was free."

The masseuse has set up her stall on the Third Floor. When I wander down there to pay for the massage she hasn't given me I spy Mary Hockaday sitting at a spare computer.

"Hello!" I say. "What are you doing here? I thought you were off to Ashridge for six months?"

She says she's had to come in to check her e-mails but she cannot do that in her office because she has officially 'left' and it now belongs to Bill Rogers. But Bill is not in his office because that film crew from *Panorama* is in there, getting ready to film Greg Dyke about the Hutton Inquiry. Which I'm sure has nothing at all to do with the Editor choosing today, of all days, to come in from leave to check her e-mails thereby risking the possibility of bumping into the Director-General in person.

———•———

Tuesday, 23 September. Bush House, Centre Block. I am standing in a trance of nostalgia, minding my own business on the wide marble staircase, gazing at the photos of Bush House under construction, 1919–1926. A new batch of them has just gone on show, dense with period detail. Bush House was built the way Broadcasting House is being demolished. There, in archival black & white, is the same giant hole in the ground, the same skeleton of steel girders …

WHACK!

Someone coming downstairs behind me claps me far too hard on the shoulder, aggressively in fact.

"Ouch!"

"Alright, Chris?"

"Who the ..?"

Mark Byford. Of course. My mate. He is stepping out to lunch with a woman sheathed in a black suit. Presumably, they are heading for some important and necessary strategic corporate discussion at taxpayers' expense.

"Cheers, Chris."

Thanks, Mark. Thanks for recognising me, old buddy. You're the dude.

—•—

Monday, 29 September. Newsroom, Centre Desk. Night shift. It is a truth universally acknowledged on the Centre Desk that celebrity deaths come in threes. While copytasting the news agencies in ENPS I notice that an obscure Caribbean politician, a former Foreign Minister of St. Lucia, one George Odlum, has died. I know then that we will be in for a couple more deaths before the night is over and check the 'Emergency Procedures' folder in case one of them should turn out to be the ailing Pope. His death has been rated as a Category A news flash – so important that it must be used to interrupt whatever programme is on air at the time. I dread being on duty when that particular crock of contents hits the fan. Within minutes, someone from the Third Floor is at my shoulder saying that Althea Gibson has died.

"Who?"

"Althea Gibson. I think we ought to do something on her …"

I apply the standard Newsroom test and throw the question open.

"Anyone here heard of Anthea Gibson?"

"Who?"

"I knew an Anthea once," says ANC suggestively.

"Althea," says our informant somewhat testily. "Al. Thea. She was the first black woman to win Wimbledon."

"Oh. In that case …"

I will never forget the trouble I got into when I spiked* the death of Curtis Mayfield on the grounds that he had never had a Number One hit. No sooner have we written a few lines on Althea Gibson than AFP flashes the news that Elia Kazan has died.

"Who?" says the new boy on attachment from Telly Centre who's riding with Centre Desk on his first pattern of Dawns.

"Elia Kazan. The Hollywood director."

"Never heard of him."

"Elia *Kazan*!"

"What did he direct, then?"

" *On the Waterfront*."

"What?"

"Eva Marie Saint. Marlon Brando. 'I coulda bin a contendah'. That one."

Everyone over 40 working on Centre Desk remembers the name Elia Kazan so into the Top he goes as a Hollywood great (director's cut). Nor is that the last of the excitement. These days, it seems, Death to comes in fours when it drops by Centre Desk in the dark hours before dawn.

CEN 0500 OLDEST MAN DIES

A retired Japanese silk-worm breeder who was believed to be the world's oldest man has died at the age of one-hundred-and-fourteen. His family said Yukichi Chuganji died of natural causes at his home in the island of Kyushu; it's also the birthplace of the world's oldest woman, Kamato Hongo, who celebrated her one-hundred-and-sixteenth birthday last Tuesday. Yukichi Chuganji graduated from technical school at the start of the last century. He drank milk every day, but did not consume alcohol.

—◦—

Thursday, 2 October. Haverstock Hill. I take the car today not the bike, arriving fresh and un-sweaty. In my head is a date for ending therapy.

"I thought maybe St. George's day. Shakespeare's birthday. The end of March. "

"How does that make you feel?" says Alan.

"Sad."

"Good."

"What?"

"What?"

"You said 'good'."

"No I didn't."

"I heard you say 'good'. You said, 'how does that feel?' And I said, 'sad'. And then you said, 'good'. It felt like you wanted to validate my sadness."

"But I didn't say 'good'. I may have made a sound, I didn't say 'good'."

⊱─━─◦─○─◦─━─⊰

Tuesday, 7 October. Newsroom, Centre Desk. The News Traffic tannoy announces Greg Dyke material coming in on channel nine. What can that be? What's our favourite top geezer been up to now? We put on our cans* to listen in. There's is nothing on channel nine except a confused hubbub of background voices. Then we hear some Cockney-style back-chat.

" 'Ow abaht this, mate, for level*? Awright? Yeah, stand there willya, right there."

That is the BBC interviewer.

"Cor, yeah. What's your first question gonna be, a load of bollocks as usual?"

And that is Greg Dyke.

He sounds exactly like someone on Centre Desk doing an impersonation of Greg Dyke. He is being interviewed at the Conservative Party annual conference about a decision to allow a merger between the two ITV companies, Carlton and Granada. At one point he says, "What? The three gorillas? That is so fuckin' boring, that is. I wish I'd never said it."

"You know, Chris," says RD, taking the cans from his ears with a perplexed look, "I really think Dyke is a bit thick. I really do. How the fuck they can let a man who talks like that become Director-General of the BBC for fucksake?"

CHAPTER EIGHT

Standing Up

Thursday, 9 October. Newsroom, Centre Desk. The Head of Radio News, Steve Mitchell, arrives to brief us all on the Hutton Inquiry. Colleagues on the Third Floor smell the beer and sandwiches and swarm up *en masse*; it's an instinct they have. I have never seen the Newsroom so full, even on the famous occasion when Mark Byford came to announce an increase in audience figures and nobody clapped at the end of it.

Steve Mitchell gives us his usual dry, self-deprecatory intro – "I thought I was coming here for a quiet chat" – and proceeds to defend the BBC by saying that Andrew Gilligan's reporting of what David Kelly told him – that the government twisted intelligence material to justify invading Iraq – was perhaps a bit suspect in its wording but that it was right for the *Today* programme to put the story in the public domain. This seems to be the gist of the BBC's defence. He then takes a few questions.

So far, I've been listening from behind my computer screen on Centre Desk so I stand up to make myself heard. At any moment I expect the News Traffic tannoy to squawk above my head and drown me out.

"I remember a phone conversation I had with you a couple of years ago, Steve, not long after Andrew Gilligan had joined the *Today* programme, when his name wasn't known at all here at Bush

House, and you said that you had recruited him with the specific brief of breaking stories that would embarrass the government. In view of what's happened with the David Kelly suicide and the row that's blown up with the government over the 'dodgy dossier' – the Hutton Inquiry – you must be pretty pleased with him?"

Someone sniggers but mostly the room seems to be hoping that I'm serious.

"I'm sure I wouldn't have put it quite as crudely as that …"

"You did actually. You put it exactly like that. I was sitting at this desk, talking to you on this phone. I can't remember exactly what the story was about, some kind of leak that Gilligan had got hold of about some Ministry of Defence spending review or something, but my point was: could we use him; was this Gilligan guy reliable? And you said, 'Of course you can use him. That's why I recruited him. Andrew's job is to come up with stories that embarrass the government, the kind of stories that will show the *Today* programme setting its own agenda ...' "

There. I've done it. Instead of writing sarcastic e-mails and not sending them I have stood up and said it. In public. With witnesses. It is a bit of a breakthrough for me from the therapeutic point of view.

>──◦──<

Friday, 10 October. Newsroom, Centre Desk. During lulls in the daily news cycle we like to sit around with our feet on the furniture, gossiping about colleagues behind their backs and swapping notes about how well things aren't going. I am thus busily engaged when someone persuades me to tell again the old, old story about COD and KAH – for the benefit of anyone who might not have heard it before.

"'What? That boring old story? I must have told everyone in the Newsroom by now."

"You haven't told me," pipes up MN.

"Right. In that case. Do you remember the days when KAH was Regional Output supremo? She was the one who decided we needed a reporter for the Africa desk. COD was quite new at the time but he was interested in the job so he sent me a message, 'What do I have to do around here to get the Africa reporter's job?' And I sent a message back saying, 'This is the BBC. If you want promotion, sleep with the boss.' And he replied saying, 'Does that mean I have to shag KAH?' and he sent it to KAH."

"No I didn't."

Great. Who should show up at the very moment when I am telling the legend but the legend himself. Yes, he says, he did send the message – but he sent it to me, CGM, not KAH.

"Oh," says MN. "That's not funny at all."

"Yes it is," says COD. "I sent that message to Chris and then I finished my shift as normal and went down to the Club for a drink and stayed too long. Next day when I came into the office I was obviously looking the worse for wear because I got a message from you, Chris, saying 'You look wrecked, what were you doing last night?' and I replied, 'I had to drink ten pints to get my courage up before shagging KAH,' and *that's* the message I sent her."

Monday, 13 October. Newsroom, Centre Desk. My new beard is getting too much attention, or is that the point? Everyone has a theory. Obviously, I am having a mid-life crisis.

"Beards happen to guys when they get to 40," asserts REM.

"In that case, I'm a bit late. I'm 48 on Friday."

"So. Forty. Fifty. Same thing. You're feeling your age."

Some people think I'm growing a beard because I want to look younger, some because I want to look older. Some think it makes me look fatter, some that it makes me look thinner. Someone comes over from *World Briefing* to stroke it for luck.

"That fucking beard, mate. What's going on?"

Probably, I am mourning the end of therapy. I am grieving in advance for the loss of Alan in my life. Alan: good dad. Greg Dyke: bad dad. I feel sorry for the BBC. I feel sorry for myself. That's why I'm growing a beard that makes my face look more like a cat's arse than Mark Thompson having a bad beard day.

⊷―◦―⊶

FROM: Bill Rogers.
SENT: Tuesday, 14 October.
TO: Band 10s.
SUBJECT: Kill Bill!

'Dear All, My apologies, but I expect by the end of this week I'll have missed every 0945 meeting. It went like this:

Monday: Steve Mitchell's management meeting – on the wider News business plan

Tuesday: Mark Byford's breakfast – focus group reports on
    Ghana and Nigeria
Wednesday: 'Leading the Way' – third meeting of 300 or so
    managers with Greg Dyke
Thursday: 'Leading the Way' – day two
Friday: BBC Pay and Grading Workshop – I'm on the UPA
    group
Fun, huh?
Bill Rogers, Managing Editor, Radio News.'

Tuesday, 21 October. To Haverstock Hill, obsessing every inch of the way. I learned last week that Greg Dyke is booked for an appearance at my Ashridge leadership course. He is bound to give us a speech and take questions afterwards. How would it be if I were to take out my yellow plastic 'Cut the Crap ' card and say "Remember this, Greg? What went wrong?" Or, "Why is it, Greg, that every time I hear the phrase 'Make it Happen' I feel like saying, 'Cut the Crap'?" Or, "I have worked for five Directors-General, Greg, and you are the first one who's ever felt the need to spell it out that he thinks the BBC is crap.' "

Alan shakes his head.

"Too rehearsed. Too personal. Keep it simple. This guy is never going to let himself be beaten in public. If you turn up with a speech in your head, or a clever script, everybody in the room is going to know where you're coming from."

"I need *some*thing. I'll be standing up again."

Isn't that the mature thing to do - to stand up, to speak out, to take responsibility? Alan strokes his thick beard.

"The point about Greg Dyke is, he is *not* your dad. Greg Dyke is not the problem. The BBC is not the problem."

Of course the BBC is not the problem. Problem-wise, in therapy, it's always about mums, dads and potty training.

"And yet Greg Dyke *is* a millionaire self-publicist. And 'Make it Happen' *is* a pointless waste of tax-payer's money…"

"Sure. But who benefits if you blast off a lot of personal *angst* at Greg Dyke for no apparent reason? Who comes out of that looking cool? One short, simple question is all you need."

><
Wednesday, 29 October. Ashridge, Buckinghamshire. I impress myself by driving the entire 50 miles without one wrong turn. An innocuous gateway leads down into a park of noble trees. The ancient house dawdles along its ridge, piled high with grey pinnacles and decorative battlements. Inside, the vault of the Ashridge's great hall soars nearly 100 feet over my head. In the wood-panelled dining room I gorge on plump sausages and sweet grilled tomatoes. Outside, aristocratic deer cast slanting shadows across the terraced lawns. I imagine myself as an Earl of Brownlow – striding my acres, hugging my trees.

Mary Hockaday addresses the assembly like a nervous Head Girl making her first speech at a prize-giving. Leadership prefects distribute folders of stationery bearing the scrupulously trendy lower-case logo of the BBC leadership programme: *ashridge.*

Overhead, a light beam projects the theme of our first day's work.

'The context of leadership within the BBC'.

The prefects stand by with marker pens at flip charts stationed around the room.

'Make it Happen'. 'One BBC'. 'Connect with Your Audience'.

We drift from one flip chart to the next like shepherd-less sheep, an audience failing to connect. There is no content, no fibre, nothing to get our teeth into. The whole event, we are told, is about tone. Managing the BBC is a life-long learning journey. Worryingly, of the four journalists in my group, each one a professional sceptic, I am the only one who says, "this is really embarrassing."

⊢•◆•○•◆•⊣

Thursday, 30 October. Ashridge. And lo, it came to pass that on the morning of the second day the top geezer, yeah, was seen about the earth, for he did come among us in his Lexus, arrayed in jeans, with the top two buttons of his shirt undone, and he did read from off his deck of index cards, and verily he did speak unto us.

"I said soon after I joined the BBC that I thought the organisation was over-managed and under-led. It all seemed terribly over-laden with bureaucracy. Originally, see, I was a programme-maker. And as a programme-maker I was responsible for a team of about 15 people. And that, I still think, is about the size of the perfect team

... Later in my career the challenge I faced was different – how to I apply the small team model of leadership to a big organisation ... When I became Chief Executive of London Weekend Television, they sent me to America to learn about business management. They sent me to the Harvard Business School and instead of the claptrap I was expecting I came across a guy called John Cotter. Let me tell you some of the things he told me.

"Leadership is more important than management. And the most important bit of it is to give your team confidence and self-belief. Many of the people working for us are better and more talented than we believe. But they're only going to achieve their best if you give them support and confidence.

"No one is indispensable. Tell the workaholics to go home. One of the things I've noticed about the BBC is that not only do you all work together, but you all go out together after work. You marry each other. You have affairs with each other. For God's sake, get out more. Get a life outside the BBC.

"I came away from John Cotter with the strong belief that you mustn't change the way you are just because you become more senior in an organisation. Don't adopt the language of management, or the language of accountants. Be yourself. Otherwise the staff will see through you.

"You cannot just be a leader, you must also manage. This includes keeping an eye on the finances. You must insist that the accountants present you with their figures in a language you can understand. Otherwise, how can you run the business?

"Value the people who work for you, and show it ... Take care

of your people ... Praise in public, coach in private ... The BBC
has been here for more than 70 years and this is the first leadership
course we have ever done. A lot was achieved in the '90s in terms of
improving the BBC's systems. But the most successful companies
during the '90s were those that cared most for their people, and
that's where I think we lost out. Any questions?"

The prefects prowl among us with microphones.

"Poor performance, Greg, how do you manage it effectively?"

"Normally, in television, you don't. You just keep telling the
talent how wonderful they are until you can't stand them any longer.
Getting rid of people in the BBC is so bureaucratic and takes so long
you can see why nobody does it."

"Work life balance – do you have a good one?"

"Yes, I think I do. But the bloke who does my garden doesn't. I
have a rule not to work at weekends. Weekends are for me and my
family. I have never met anyone who said on his death bed, I wished
I had spent more time at the office."

"Charter Review – how's it going?"

"One of the things that struck me about the BBC when I joined it
was, how do I judge this organisation? I mean, it's not a profit and
loss thing. When I joined the BBC we had spent the past decade
worrying about what the politicians thought of us. Now I think we
are worried about what the audience thinks of us, and I think that's
right. We will be judged as successful if our audience like us."

And that is nearly it. The hour that Greg can spare the BBC
leadership programme is almost up. I raise my hand but someone
else gets the microphone and launches into a long, blundering, badly

rehearsed question that reveals how bitter he is about his lack of career advancement. By the time his question had been dealt with – quite kindly – there is barely time for my own.

"Greg, as Editor-in-Chief of the BBC what could you have done to stop the Andrew Gilligan row with the government getting so dangerously out of hand?"

"When I look back on those days straight after the Gilligan report went out there are things we could and should have done differently. I think the government, Alastair Campbell, was gunning for the BBC. And they had a large section of the press on their side. We had to stand up to that. But we could have done things to calm it down. We could have offered to have an internal inquiry. There was a stage when we could have said: Look, okay, we seem to have made a mistake, someone's cocked up somewhere, we'll have a full internal inquiry. But that's with hindsight. All you can do at the time is back your people. We pay people to make judgements and sometimes they get it wrong. People make mistakes. But I can tell you this: the Gilligan story is right. Once you've seen all the stuff, there's no doubt that Gilligan's story is right. The government did sex up that dossier about Iraqi weapons. So we were right to report it. But we probably made a few mistakes along the way. You've just got to get on with it, that's all."

After lunch I find myself in a different group of collaborators from the one I started out with. One of the new guys is a member of Greg Dyke's Executive Committee. One member is supposed to attend every Ashridge course and this guy is our particular Exco rep. So I ask him about Greg Dyke and John Cotter and how it really is at the top of the BBC.

"Er …" he says, avoiding eye contact. "I think, yeah, Greg does kind of, like, try to be that way. But it's like, the BBC's a huge organisation … So … "

Mr Exco definitely does not want to talk. My new collaborators are embarrassed. I can tell they want me to shut up right now and piss on someone else's 'break-out group'. I slink off to my room to carry on reading the biography of Lord Kitchener I found in the library last night. Apparently, he was staying at Ashridge with the Brownlows when news reached him about the outbreak of the First World War.

<hr />

Sunday, 2 November. Newsroom, Centre Desk. 'Make it Happen' has happened with a vengeance while I was away with the deer polishing up my leadership techniques. Someone has scrapped all the drawers. Why? No one knows.

Once upon a time in the Newsroom there were drawers for all, in handy little units on wheels that could be slipped under any desk. Handy, that is, for keeping stuff in. Now they are gone, except for the drawers under the SDE's desk where the precious key to the stationery cupboard is stored. It's a mystery, as Toyah Willcox used to say. And the stuff that used to be kept in those handy drawers – historic *diktats* and important policy memos – is now lying around all over the Newsroom, waiting for the cleaners.

We think we are special but we're not. We think that because we apply ourselves with care and due diligence to the task of telling the world its news hour by hour that the World Service is important and worthwhile. We are deluding ourselves. All jobs are the same.

Each day in the Newsroom starts with ID cards and security checks. We sit under neon lights that are never switched off, day or night. On one side we look down into the Bush House car park. From the opposite windows we can see into the offices at the back of the Australian High Commission on the other side of Melbourne Place. Room 440, S.E. Wing, is our precise postal address and it's just like any other open-plan office in London. We sit in front of a computer screen. Everyone has a phone on the desk. Information as a commodity is fed to us and we turn it into news and send it on its way. Our vended coffee tastes of metal if it doesn't end up on our shoes. Our highly trained leaders delegate blame downwards and keep the interesting decisions to themselves while paying themselves bonuses every year for doing a grand job. And then one day they take our drawers away, which leaves us wondering …

Tuesday, 4 November. Haverstock Hill. Alan wouldn't be human if, having given me specific advice about how to tackle Greg Dyke, he didn't want to know what happened when I stood up to speak.

"So. Was his answer to your question a good one?"

"Very good. He came across as a decent kind of bloke, a real diamond geezer."

How badly do I need a bad dad in my life? How much longer do I need to hold on to what is holding me back? Ashridge has left me feeling unsettled. I adored the old house and the autumn trees but came away as confused as ever about the BBC and me. I can never re-illusion myself, that's the problem. It's no use Greg Dyke being a decent bloke underneath, if that's what he is, because I am too tainted by experience to re-illusion myself.

⊢•◆─○─◆•⊣

Saturday, 8 November. Newsroom, Centre Desk. The annual BBC Staff Survey arrives requiring me to respond to the usual questions. Yes, I would be critical of the BBC without being asked. No, I strongly disagree that people here trust each other. Yes, I strongly agree that there is too much change for change's sake. No, I strongly disagree that people are selected for jobs based on their skills, knowledge and experience. Yes, I strongly agree that I have been doing these surveys for years and it's still getting worse …

⊢•◆─○─◆•⊣

Sunday, 16 November. Newsroom, Centre Desk. Newsroom Log.

> 'Canteen Trays. Many thanks for complying with the new Catering Policy by not removing cutlery & crockery from the canteen … I've fed back views we've had about plastic knives not being strong enough to cut some items of food … We've done well with the food & cutlery. But as there are no plans to introduce tray recovery here's a plea to keep the flow of trays returning to the Lower Ground floor where they belong …'

⊢•◆─○─◆•⊣

FROM: Chris Moore, SDE.
TO: Jackie Leonard, newsreader.
SENT: 24 November.
SUBJECT: 'Children in Need'

'Jackie, As part of our fun participation in "Children in Need" we have had to re-configure your next hourly time-check as follows:

The time in Lagos is 14 hours, in Rio it's four o' clock and in Aleksandra Bokovicha-Cherkassago it's six in the morning and very cold indeed. Wherever you are, whatever you're doing, the bosses of the BBC want to look good by raising loads of dosh for "Children in Need" so welcome, I'm Jackie Leonard and these are the BBC news headlines:

Staff at the BBC World Service have bid nothing for the chance to attend a business breakfast with Mark Byford to celebrate "Children in Need" day.

A charity auction of draft policy initiatives drawn up for "Children in Need" day by Phil Harding has been cancelled due to lack of interest.

The managing editor of World Service News and Current Affairs has been taken to hospital after spraining both wrists during a sponsored collect-a-tray marathon intended to raise money for "Children in Need".

Later in the programme we'll be catching up with the international response to "Children in Need" but first …

over the Newsroom for the usual round up of bits and pieces cobbled together from the news wires …'

CHAPTER NINE

How To Achieve Nothing By Not Shouting

Tuesday, 25 November. Henry Wood House, Portland Place, London W1. I must have passed this place more than a thousand times but I never knew it belonged to the BBC. Waiting inside is a Human Resources* specialist.

"Hi!" says Pam brightly. "Glad you could make it. How about a coffee?"

Pam has been primed to brief me on the results of the 360 degree survey I completed as part of the Ashridge leadership course. She says I am the kind of manager who can resolve conflict effectively, who promotes the values of the BBC, who challenges the prejudices of others and fosters creativity and divergent thinking, all of which are excellent leadership qualities. But. I am not so good at building productive relationships across the BBC nor at managing efficiently against budgets.

"Maybe that's because I don't have a budget."

"None at all?" says Pam doubtingly.

"I have purposely managed my career to avoid anything to do with budgets."

"Ah."

I don't wear a pager on my belt. I don't have a mobile phone. On my days off I want everyone to know that I am off. Is it possible that Pam has never met a dinosaur before?

I explain my routine as an SDE on the Centre Desk rota.

"I cycle to work, fiddle with the headlines, eat my sandwiches, go to a second-hand bookshop in my lunch hour and then cycle home again after handing over my bulletin to someone else who doesn't wear a pager or manage a budget. After four days of doing that I get four days off – whoopee!"

"It suggests here," says Pam, "that your priority areas for development might include 'collaborating across boundaries' and 'using external thinking'."

She peeks at me through her mascara.

"How does that resonate with you?"

Through the window behind Pam's head, on the other side of Portland Place, are the sixth-floor windows of the Langham Hotel. When I joined the BBC the Langham belonged to the BBC and behind that row of windows was a low-ceilinged room where once a week journalism trainees were given lessons in T-line shorthand – me, Jana, Lorraine, the Pesch, Torquil, Kirsty, Julie and Anne. The courteous woman who used to teach us shorthand was called Florence and she lived in Great Missenden, Bucks. And she had a luscious secretary to help her, and her secretary was called … Patience ..? Princesse ..?

"When the Langham Hotel belonged to the BBC, Pam, it had a big lift in the lobby, made of wood inlaid with beautiful marquetry. An old man with a peaked cap sat inside it on a wooden stool. He was employed full-time by the BBC to drive that antique lift up and down all day long."

Pam looks at me as if I have lost the plot, which I don't think I have.

"Up. Down. Up. Down. Four days on. Four days off. Four on, four off …"

Our work at the British Broadcasting Corporation is to shift the commodity from one place to another. In my case the commodity is news. I will be shifting it up and down, Third Floor, Fourth Floor, days on, days off, until the day comes when I decide to take redundancy or BBC News decides to wield the hatchet. It's work. It's how I pay my mortgage and earn my pension. From the expression on Pam's face I can tell my analysis quite fails to resonate.

‹—•—○—•—›

Wednesday, 26 November. Newsroom, Centre Desk. The front page of *Ariel* says this week's telethon for the charity 'Children in Need' raised £15 million.

> 'A week in Dyke's luxury flat went for £1,300 and Chairman
> Gavyn Davies outbid the DG to pay an astounding £11,000 for
> a signed David Beckham Real Madrid football shirt.'

No one seems to care that the governance of the BBC has been entrusted to plutocrats who think it's a good afternoon's lark to blow £11,000 on a signed football shirt. On the other hand, £15,000,000 for charity is an indisputably good thing so stop your stupid, negative sarcasm, you grouchy whingeing whinger. Why do you have to be so negative all the time? Cut the Crap and Make it Happen. You might enjoy it. Ha ha.

Friday, 28 November. Newsroom, Centre Desk. The lead story when we take over from the early shift has put the whole of Bush House into a stupor – something about the Taiwanese parliament passing a law allowing the government to hold referendums on changes to the constitution. At the 1600 editorial meeting I learn that the Africans are leading with a story about Congo and the Latinos with something about Brazil, and quite right too. The whole of Centre Desk agrees that we need some breaking news right now. Rarely do the gods of the Newsroom answer our prayers so promptly. The outgoing shift has hardly finished packing its bags before I am reaching for the tannoy.

"*Bing-bong!* Hello, Newsroom. There's a new lead story coming. We're snapping it right now ..."

President Bush has flown 7000 miles to Baghdad in secret. He has served up some Thanksgiving turkey to his troops, delivered a speech about freedom and democracy and flown home again without anyone knowing a thing about it. We feel truly thankful.

>---◦---<

Wednesday, 3 December. Newsroom, Centre Desk. I collect my new BBC diary for next year from the box of free diaries outside Tithers' office. The cover for the Year 2004 looks a right old mess with the key Dykeist buzz words blazoned at random across it: Trust; Audiences; Quality; Working Together. I try to scratch them out but the biro won't bite.

>---◦---<

Tuesday, 9 December. Newsroom, Centre Desk. Night shift. The back page of *Ariel* has launched a new column called *Greg's Gags* with a picture of the man himself, laughing at his own jokes, har har, pull the other one, know what I mean, up the Khyber. Unfortunately, none of them are gags, so far as I can make out.

- Greg asked Southampton season ticket holder and BBC chairman Gavyn Davis [sic] if he'd like to join his party in a private box for the FA Cup Final. 'No thanks, I like to take my family to football like ordinary fans,' the chairman told him. 'How are you getting there?' Greg inquired. 'Oh, in my private plane …'
- Greg bought a pile of digital radios to give as Christmas presents at the BBC shop in The Forum, BBC East's new HQ in Norwich. He thought he'd got an amazing deal. 'More amazing than you know,' said someone in the know in Norwich. 'You can't receive anything on them!' Happily the digital transmitter for the area was switched on two weeks ago.

I mean, what kind of gag is that?

- Here's how the DG fared under quick-fire questioning from Jeremy Vine. Q: 6pm Radio 4 news *vs* 6pm TV news? A: Depends where you are. Q: Wogan *vs* Sara Cox? A: Neither. Q: When did you last listen to Radio 3? A: Don't remember. Q: Alan Green: genius or pub bore? A: A bit of both. Q: Brian Perkins? A: No comment. Q: If *Woman's Hour* and Five Live had an arm wrestling contest, who would win? A: *Woman's Hour*. Five Live wouldn't stand a chance.

These are not gags. They're anecdotes. And they're not totally hilarious. Is it *Ariel* again, sucking up to 'Make it Happen'? Or is it just me again – whingeing on until everyone has left the room out of sheer boredom?

◦—◦—◦—◦—◦

FROM: Greg Dyke.

SENT: 10 December 2003.

SUBJECT: Mark Byford to become Deputy Director-General.

'This email is going to all staff.

Later this morning I plan to announce that Mark Byford will become Deputy Director-General from January. He will report to me and deputise for me when I'm away … Anyone who knows or has worked with Mark appreciates what a passionate advocate he is for public service broadcasting and for the BBC's role both in the UK and around the world so I'm delighted that the Governors have agreed his appointment … In the New Year, we will appoint a new Director of the World Service … Yours, Greg.'

◦—◦—◦—◦—◦

FROM: Mark Byford & PA.

SENT: 10 December 2003.

SUBJECT: To all staff in the Global Division.

'Dear Colleague, Further to Greg's announcement today of my appointment as Deputy Director General from January, here are some further details … As Deputy Director General, I will continue to head the Global News Division with overall responsibility for BBC World Service … I'll also remain the Accounting Officer to the Foreign Office for the grant-in-aid funding … Thank you for your support. I'm very proud and privileged to become the BBC's Deputy Director General. I'm also really pleased to retain my leadership role of the Global News Division. Regards, Mark.'

⊢•⧫•○•⧫•⊣

Sunday, 14 December. Home Desk, London SW4. I have just got up from sleeping off my night shift when there's a call from the sitting room.

"They've captured Saddam Hussein."

The telly shows the once-mighty fugitive dictator in the guise of a sad old tramp (wild hair, matted beard) being searched for lice by an American military medic. I thank my lucky stars I am nowhere near Centre Desk at this precise moment. The leadership will be phoning in every ten minutes with helpful suggestions. When I go in to the kitchen to hear what the World Service Newsroom has managed to crank up on the story it sounds pretty lame. Radio news always sounds lame when the only audio available is telly without the pictures.

⊢•⧫•○•⧫•⊣

Wednesday, 17 December. Ashridge, Buckinghamshire. I arrive on schedule in time for lunch followed by a stroll among the sequoias, the mighty cedars and the great oak planted by the young Queen

Victoria. I love them all. I also have a soft spot for the rose bower where George Nathaniel Curzon is alleged to have proposed, one perfumed summer night in the Edwardian long ago, to the American heiress who became his bride. After that it is straight into another afternoon of group discussions, Post-It notes and Death by Flip Chart, during which I learn that our former Exco collaborator has left the BBC quietly and without fanfare which might explain his former reticence about Greg Dyke's leadership qualities. At teatime I take to my bed to try to sleep off the usual Awayday migraine.

><+>-0-<+><

Friday, 19 December. Ashridge. Day Two. A gorgeous sight greets me when I walk into the grand, panelled dining room for breakfast. Outside the French windows where the sun's rays strike the white-frosted lawns a translucent mist is rising. Within this cloud move the ethereal shapes of the estate's deer grazing in three dimensions. After such a beautiful start, it's downhill all the way. More flip-charts. More group discussion. More feedback. My group of collaborators finds itself signing up for some 'Action Learning', in other words group therapy, at a date to be arranged somewhere in London. I tell the facilitator I'm willing to sign up to anything that doesn't require written homework on my days off.

><+>-0-<+><

FROM: Chris Hipwell.
SENT: 04 January 2004.
SUBJECT: BBC Response to 'Independent' story on Stephen Mitchell.

'This email is being sent to everyone in News, and shortly to senior managers across the BBC

Message from Richard Sambrook, Director, News: You may have seen press reports about possible consequences of the Hutton enquiry. I am enclosing a letter I sent today to the Editor of the *Independent on Sunday* correcting completely false speculation ...

Your article, "BBC lines up news chief as Hutton fall guy" (*Independent on Sunday*, 4 January 2004) is plain wrong. It is simply not true that Stephen Mitchell, or anyone else, is being identified as a fall guy after the Hutton Inquiry reports ... Stephen Mitchell is a much admired and trusted figure within the Corporation. Yours sincerely, Richard Sambrook.'

———◦———

Sunday, 4 January 2004. Newsroom, Centre Desk. Hold the front page. The Newsroom night shift is rocked to its foundations. The Editor is having another baby. If it's worth knowing MAC is usually the first to know it.

"This isn't one of your jokes is it?"

MAC says the news comes straight from an unimpeachable senior source.

"The plan is for Mary to start her next maternity leave as soon as she finishes at Ashridge."

"Nice timing."

Someone wonders aloud if Mary ever really wanted the Editor's job or only the promotion. Either way seems fair to me. By the time she comes back, if she does come back, her *curriculum vitae* will show that she's been Editor for about three years; in fact, she will have sat in the chair for a not much more than about half that. I tell everyone that I wouldn't be surprised if Mary decides to stay at Ashridge. They can't take the SPS grade away from her and Mary & Co. hasn't crashed in flames during her absence. The Newsroom runs itself, like the rest of the BBC. Three-quarters of the SPS cadre could be sent to Ashridge permanently and no one would know the difference.

⊢•⊶•⊸•⊶•⊣

Tuesday, 6 January. Newsroom, Centre Desk. Night shift. Noisy disagreements with BBC Newsgathering all night. When the Americans drop a robotic space probe on Mars, CNN takes us live to mission control in Pasadena. As soon as those dudes in short-sleeves start whooping and punching the air we put out the story.

SNAP MARS LANDING

Some news just in … A sophisticated robotic vehicle aimed at exploring Mars has landed on the planet. Mission controllers at the American space agency NASA cheered as the craft made its first impact. Later, they lost signal while the machine bounced to a final halt.

The Intake editor is away from her desk at the time so it falls to her assistant to try to raise something from the correspondent sent by Telly Centre to cover the story. The Intake assistant establishes contact and says our correspondent doesn't intend to file a piece.

"Why not?"

"She says she doesn't want to report a successful landing because there's been no signal from the robot. The guys in Pasadena are still waiting to hear a signal."

"We know that. We've seen the pictures. All she has to do is report what we've seen – the touchdown, the cheering, the lack of signal. That's the news. We need a generic minute."

"Oh! She's gone."

"Well get her back please."

The Intake assistant raises the correspondent's producer. Yes comes the response, a generic minute will be forthcoming.

"Thank you."

At about 0450 hours, the telly shows us more cheering and hollering over in Pasadena. They've got a signal from the robot. Thank you, CNN. We prepare another snap.

SECOND SNAP MARS LANDING

In the last few moments, a signal has been received from the landing on the surface of Mars. A controller in California described it as a very strong signal.

The time is now 0452 GMT. Centre Desk has eight minutes to wrap the two snaps into a story, to re-write the Top, to re-write the Summary and to re-order the bulletin running order. Nobody notices the ominous silence from Pasadena until it's too late.

"Where's the correspondent?"

"Doing a two-way* with Five Live."

"I didn't hear that on Traffic."

"They've had technical problems in Pasadena. The correspondent didn't come up through Traffic. She went straight through to Five Live on mobile."

So that's how the BBC World Service bulletin covers the Mars landing story – with our two snaps written together and 15 seconds of random hooting and hollering. Traffic does not announce the arrival of our correspondent's generic minute until 0502 hours, exactly one minute too late. The Intake assistant looks at me apologetically. It's not her fault.

"Who's on duty at Telly Centre tonight?"

Sensing that something unpleasant might be about to happen the Intake assistant goes off to track down the Intake editor. By the time they return I am on the phone to Newsgathering.

"We're just wondering here at Bush why we didn't get a generic minute from Pasadena."

"That's a good question. That's what we're asking ourselves right now."

"Well what's the answer? Did you send a correspondent to Pasadena to report the news or to fanny about on the mobile all night?"

"You're not going to achieve anything by shouting."

"Actually, as everyone can hear, I am not shouting. Where was our generic minute?"

"Shouting won't get you anywhere."

"I'm not shouting. But I'll tell you what I am – sick and tired of trying to make radio news without any of the generic minutes we've been promised."

Wednesday, 6 January. Haverstock Hill. I am struck by a moment of insight – I've had enough. It's the same old things coming round and round again. That's why I am ending therapy. I see Ashridge in my mind's eye.

"At this country house I told you about, where the BBC leadership course was held, on the last day, as I was leaving, I noticed a vista through the trees and at the end of it was an obelisk. So instead of heading straight for the motorway, I took a detour and drove over for a closer look. I had assumed that this obelisk thing would be a memorial to the estate workers who'd died in the Great War, 1914–1918, but it was a monument to some Earl's dead wife."

Matters of life and death will never stop coming round and round. Get used to it. Love the ones you love, including yourself, before you die.

"Yeah, I think I know that place," says Alan, "that view through the trees. What's it called that place? It's north of Hemel …"

Ashridge is north of Hemel Hempstead.

"That's it," says Alan. "I used to take the dog there."

He is my favourite substitute dad. I imagine Alan fondly in his boots and anorak, scuffling through the autumn leaves with his dog scampering ahead. I see him kicking hairy beech nuts at the squirrels. Good place for a dog, the woods around Ashridge.

"He was a big Labrador," says Alan. "He could really go for it up there. He loved it. He used to put his head down and run like the wind. He's dead now."

CHAPTER TEN

Downfall

Monday, January 12. Newsroom, Centre Desk. On my first daylight shift of this new year. Tithers summons his Band 10s to a confidential, closed-door briefing in his corner office. Whatever the secret, it must be big; the Tith has never taken us into his confidence like this before. Guess what, folks? The Editor is having another baby! It's due to coincide with the end of her attachment at Ashridge! She will not be coming back to Bush House before going on maternity leave!

"Nice timing."

Tithers then tells us that this time the surrogate leadership of Bill Rogers will not be required by Mary & Co. While Mary is away on maternity leave her functions will be shared between him and Liliane. This is good news, from the Diversity angle, but Liliane knows even less than Mary about news (as opposed to Current Affairs) and has never been shy of telling folk what she thinks about the Newsroom's influence in setting the department's editorial agenda. Anyone who thinks that, taking all things into consideration, the Newsroom usually manages to handle the news pretty well is not singing from the Liliane Landor hymn-sheet. She did once complete a token attachment on a regional desk in the Newsroom but it barely lasted a matter of weeks.

The prescribed function of the World Service is to provide a broad and balanced view of world events as seen from London, which is why, for decades, all of our news bulletins were introduced with the clarion call of the military march, *Lilibulero*, and the sonorous declaration: "This is London". As a self-identified outsider Liliane brings a foreign perspective to British values, which is good. She is lively, personable, a good questioner and a 'good listener'. But French is her mother tongue and writing in English has never been her strong point which is probably why, when she flitted through the Newsroom, she made sure to stay well out of range of Centre Desk.

Tithers, having brought us into his confidence and outlined the re-shuffle ahead moves on to announce that the job of deputy Tith will soon be boarded for real. BR was appointed last time on a one-year attachment. This time it will be permanent. Any questions?

It came out before I could stop it.

"Steve, what's the back-up plan if Liliane decides to get herself pregnant while Mary's on maternity leave?"

⊢⊷⊶⊙⊷⊶⊣

Monday, 19 January. Newsroom, Centre Desk. Right at the end of a dull shift at 1655 hours, with only one bulletin left, BR pays a visit to Centre Desk.

"Chris, I think it's time to get rid of the tax inspector headline."

I call it up on my screen.

'A tax inspector has been found dead at his desk but it was two days before anyone noticed.'

"But it's the only story in the bulletin anyone will remember."

"It's too tabloid," says BR. "It's been there for three hours, that's enough."

Wednesday, 21 January. Newsroom, Centre Desk. Phil Harding attends the 0900 editorial meeting, full of ideas about our inherited lead story from the Dawn shift – the last State of the Union address from President Bush before this year's U.S. election. Every BBC correspondent in Washington filed on the speech during the night. No one has filed anything since. That, I suggest, should be our first priority – to work up some American and world reaction and make that our angle into the story.

"And somebody in the Newsroom," says Harding, "should dredge through the entire speech for any other issues that haven't been covered."

Perhaps he has been away from daily news for so long he has forgotten how to do it? The State of the Union story is eight hours old. We are well beyond the dredging phase. The requirement now is to spin the story forward not load it with stinking sludge.

⊢•⊷•❍•⊶•⊣

Friday, 23 January. To Telly Centre for the closing day of the latest 'Making it Happen' charade in BBC News. Our bosses at Telly Centre are desperate to be seen to be taking 'Make it Happen' seriously so everyone who goes along on an off day can claim a whole day-off in lieu. The first session is about Diversity.

'The BBC – Still Hideously White?'

I dutifully ask the question about discrimination based on class prejudice that NOD asked me to ask on his behalf ('Black and Asian faces reading the news on telly doesn't mean they're not all middle class wankers, does it?') and hope he is listening on the ringmain* in Bush House. The whole event is being streamed around BBC News for the benefit of those working their shifts.

Afterwards I drift into to a session about what it's like to be a news cameraman at war.

"Sure it's dangerous," says the cameraman, after watching some of his video clips with us. "I do it because I love it."

As soon as some nibbles are made available I nibble some of them and bunk off into the rain, stopping at a few bookshops on the way home.

⊢⊶⊙⊷⊣

Monday, 26 January. Newsroom, Centre Desk. Night shift. An important message flashes up as soon as I log on to ENPS: advice from high up about the imminent publication of Lord Hutton's report on the BBC and its reporting of Tony Blair's allegedly dodgy Intelligence dossier that preceded the war in Iraq. In the event of a leak of the Hutton Report appearing in any of tomorrow's newspapers I should consult an executive at Telly Centre called Roger Mosey before writing any kind of story.

The early edition of *The Sun* duly arrives with the leaked Hutton Report splashed all over it. I phone Roger Mosey. He tells me to phone Stephen Mitchell. He tells me to treat it like any other story, on its merits, which is what I could already be doing if no one had delayed the process by instructing me to phone Roger Mosey. Tithers phones in from home to find out what the *The Sun* is saying so I read out the gist of it: Lord Hutton thinks that the BBC acted well dodgy from beginning to end and Greg Dyke and his senior management are to blame.

"And what about the government side?"

The BBC was expecting a rap over the knuckles from Lord Hutton but - and this is the bit no one is going to like: - he has decided that Tony Blair is cleaner than clean, that his Minister of Defence, Geoff Hoon, is squeaky clean and that his favourite spin-doctor, Alastair Campbell, is un-spotted by any taint. The balance of opinion in the Newsroom is that these findings represent a not very subtle attempt to punish the BBC for embarrassing the government over its preparations for war in Iraq. I think m'lud is being rather harsh on the *Today* programme but I also think that, as a corporate entity, the BBC has been against the war in Iraq from the start and BBC News has not been as impartial as it should have been. Not that it will make any difference. The Governors will set up a committee to look at Lord Hutton's findings and after a couple of months it will be back to business as usual.

<hr>

Tuesday, 27 January. Home, London SW4. I am pottering around in the kitchen in my nightshirt, having lately arisen from slumber, when I put on the *PM* programme on Radio 4 for a brief-up on the news. The presenter, Eddie Mair, is spluttering on about Gavyn Davies having resigned as Chairman of the BBC's Board of Governors. The actual Hutton Report has been published and it says what *The Sun* said it would say. It is a complete let-off for the government and a kick in the teeth for the BBC and BBC News in particular.

I arrive at Centre Desk for my night shift to find an e-mail waiting from Greg Dyke. He praises Gavyn Davies for taking the rap and quitting his job like a top geezer should. I am so incensed by his complacency I dash off a reply before I have even read-in.

'Dear Greg, First you said we were over-managed and under-led. Then you called us hideously white. Later, you invented a new slogan and spent millions of pounds promoting it: Cut the Crap, Make it Happen. At no stage did you make the BBC's journalism a priority. Everyone in BBC News is now paying the price of your neglect. The Hutton report damns you and your methods. Please do the decent thing and resign as soon as practicable ...'

I show it to SMJ. As usual he tells me not to send it which, as usual, I don't.

"Dyke's in a corner," he says. "What benefit are you going to get by poking him?"

He's quite right. No one benefits. But perhaps a nudge in the right direction wouldn't do any harm. It's fine and dandy for Davies to take the rap but it's Greg who's the Editor-in-Chief. Lord Hutton calls Andrew Gilligan's report about the dodgy dossier on the *Today* programme 'unfounded'. He says the BBC's system of editorial control is 'defective'. And he says the BBC's governors were 'slow to respond'. In the face of this verdict, the entire leadership of BBC News (prop. G. Dyke) appears to have collapsed into headless chicken mode.

I notice, not for the first time, that the best way to watch telly news in order to get to the heart of any story is to watch without sound. There are hardly any pictures to be seen of Lord Hutton but plenty of Greg Dyke, Gavyn Davies, Tony Blair and Alistair Campbell. This whole dodgy dossier affair is a playground brawl and Greg has come off the worst.

⊢•◆•○•◆•⊣

Wednesday, 28 January. Home Desk, London SW4. I am making a cup of tea in my nightshirt when my wife comes into the kitchen.

"Guess what's happened?"

"What?"

"Guess who's resigned this time?"

"Er. Greg Dyke?"

"Correct."

"Bloody hell!"

I turn on the radio and there's Eddie Mair again, telling us how "shocked and stunned" BBC staff have been left by Greg Dyke's resignation. Some staff at White City, where 'Make it Happen' is based, have left their offices to chant pro-Dyke slogans for the benefit of their colleagues in other media who've been tipped off about the stunt. I hear a sound-bite of Greg boasting about a deluge of e-mails urging him not to quit.

It seems there was a huge argument between Greg and the BBC Governors over the wording of the BBC's post-Hutton apology to Tony Blair and Alastair Campbell. Dyke seemingly refused to go along with the wording the governors wanted. The apology that was eventually read out by the BBC Vice-Chairman, Richard Ryder, was offered "unreservedly" and covered "all our mistakes".

It is difficult for anyone who's got anything to do with BBC News to listen to Ryder's apology without squirming with embarrassment. BBC News has been humiliated. In the meantime, Mark Byford, has been made acting Director-General. His moment has arrived. When I get to Bush House for my night shift I find a message in my inbox.

FROM: Greg Dyke.
SENT: 29 January 2004.
SUBJECT: I'm Leaving.

'This email's going to all staff.

This is the hardest e-mail I've ever written. In a few minutes I'll be announcing to the outside world that I'm leaving after four years as Director General. I don't want to go and I'll miss everyone here hugely … We need closure. We need closure to protect the future of the BBC, not for you or me but for the benefit of everyone out there. It might sound pompous but I believe the BBC really matters … The BBC has always been a great organisation but I hope that, over the last four years, I've helped to make it a more human place where everyone who works here feels appreciated … This might sound a bit schmaltzy but I really will miss you all … Yours, Greg.'

Even telly networks like CNN and Al Jazeera are carrying the story of Greg Dyke's downfall. One video clip shows Mark Byford being introduced to staff at Telly Centre while standing over a decidedly glum-looking Richard Sambrook. As the two of them go into Richard's office for an 'honest conversation' I notice Byford perform a piece of body language that I have never seen before. He makes as if to fold his arms defensively across his chest but realises in doing so that his much shorter colleague will get a negative message so changes the gesture into a sort of two-armed downward sweep as if to cover his testicles with both hands. I'm glad Mark's been made acting Director-General. Everyone will now get a chance to see for themselves what he's like.

⊷⊶○⊷⊶

Friday, 30 January. Home Desk, London SW4. On the last *PM* programme of the week, Eddie Mair is interviewing Mark Byford. Eddie reads out the unreserved apology that Richard Ryder made yesterday and asks Mark the direct question.

"What exactly is the BBC apologising for?"

"The BBC is apologising for the errors that it made."

"But which errors – the errors that the BBC admitted it made, that Greg Dyke has already apologised for, or for the errors that Lord Hutton said it made?"

"The errors that have been made by the BBC and for which it has apologised."

"But which errors?"

"What I'm saying," says Mark Byford, "is that the BBC has made mistakes and that it has apologised for these mistakes, and that in admitting its mistakes it has apologised for them and that now is the time to move forward."

"But which errors? The BBC has already apologised for Andrew Gilligan's report so what 'mistakes' are covered by the 'unreserved' apology?"

"I've told you. Lord Hutton has published his report and the BBC accepts that Lord Hutton has published its [sic] report and that it has made mistakes and that it apologises for its mistakes and that what I'm saying now is that now is the time to move forward."

He sounds like a badly wired robot with a circuit loose. My wife starts doing Dalek impersonations around the kitchen.

"It. Is. Time to. Move forward. We must move forward. We have made mis. Takes. The BBC have Made. Miss. Forward. For. Ward."

>—◦—◦—◦—<

Saturday, 31 January. Newsroom, Centre Desk. The newspapers are exploiting Greg Dyke's downfall to give the BBC a mauling. Some are describing the Hutton Report as the blackest moment in BBC history. They are also gleefully speculating about the runners and riders in the forthcoming BBC Director-General Handicap Hurdle Stakes.

The Guardian. Mark Byford: 'leading internal candidate'; Michael Jackson 'passionate about public service TV'; Mark Thompson 'cards close to his chest'; Dawn Airey 'too much of a populist'.

Daily Express. Mark Byford 2:1; Jana Bennett 3:1; Mark Thompson 4:1; Robert Kilroy- Silk: 500:1

The Independent. Mark Byford: 'bluff Yorkshireman'; Jenny Abramsky 'too old'; Jana Bennett 'retains an American accent'; Mark Thompson 'might impress'.

Sky News. Mark Byford; Mark Thompson; Jana Bennett.

The Times. Mark Byford 'question mark over his wider television experience'; Jana Bennett 'strong lobby for first female D-G'; Mark Thompson 'accused broadcasters of producing dull, mechanical and samey television'; Michael Jackson 'turned down ITV chief executive job last year'.

Mark Byford will not win the race because of the well known fact that the person chosen to plug the gap during a crisis is always discarded once it's over. Jana will not get the job because she is identified as a Dyke loyalist and there isn't enough time for her to distance herself from his legacy. Also, I'm not sure she would want the hassle. Mark Thompson will not get the job because the first thing the women on the selection board will notice when he walks if for the interview is that he's got cat fluff stuck to his face. Dawn Airey will not get it because she is far too loud and sure of herself. Jenny 'Too Old' Abramsky might make a good D-G, but she's not glamorous enough, having spent her career in radio. That leaves Michael Jackson. He is the only candidate I haven't met personally but he's in the right place at the right time – 6,000 miles away from the BBC as it grapples with the Hutton Report.

Monday, 2 February. Haverstock Hill. Another 1700 session. I arrive early and kill time in a coffee shop with the newspapers. They're still full of Greg Dyke and what will happen to the Beeb without him. Nothing, of course. *The Guardian* says Jana Bennett and Lorraine Heggessy joined the 'Greg Don't Go' demonstrations at White City last week which, if true, should scupper their chances of replacing him.

"So," says Alan. "Does Dyke's departure count as a victory?"

It certainly does, at least in the sense that he was a bad bargain for the BBC and the British tax payer. Mark Byford is still there, of course, but probably not for much longer. I think he's the type who will leave when he gets passed over for the top job despite his frequently quoted remark about "loving the BBC to bits". Alan says that when he saw Byford speaking on telly he thought he was looking at some sort of BBC clone. It does feel weird to see the main actors in my hitherto private psycho-drama performing for the whole world to judge.

Tuesday, 3 February. Newsroom Band 10s Awayday, Royal Society of Arts. The highlight of the day comes while we're discussing the merits and de-merits of individuals in the Newsroom. Every so often we take a look at the staffing across the Newsroom rota with a view to re-distributing the talent more fairly. Some SDEs are better than others at enticing the more experienced and reliable writers onto their teams.

"The thing about PAN," someone says, "is that his English still isn't quite up to the job. He puts words in the wrong place. I can't feel confident about him as a writer."

"Exactly which words," I ask, "is PAN not using properly?"

"Well. He seems to have a lot of trouble with 'the'. Sometimes he puts a 'the' where it isn't needed and doesn't put it where it is needed."

"What about 'a'. How is he with 'a'?"

"Same thing. 'A' is a problem too. He's just not sure when it's needed."

Here is someone being paid £30,000 a year by the BBC to do journalism for the World Service who cannot be trusted with 'a' and 'the'. Unfortunately, as someone points out, PAN performs well at boards and we no longer put applicants through the Newsroom Test because of Diversity and Fair Selection pressures. Instead of tests we how have to take it for granted that any journalist working for the BBC can distinguish between the definite and indefinite article whether that's the case or not. Which means PAN will be the very difficult candidate to turn down when a next promotion comes up.

CHAPTER ELEVEN

Taking The Legacy Forward

Wednesday, 4 February. White City, London W12. Welcome to the BBC's Broadcast Centre. It is a big glass box adjacent to the A4 flyover with lots of space inside and 100 pairs of shoes hanging from strings in the foyer. The shoes have been donated by BBC staff to symbolise the journeys they have made. Yes, it's an *installation*. The Action Learning takes place upstairs in a glass-walled room on the third floor with exciting floor-to-ceiling views of the traffic streaming in out of London towards the M4.

"This is exactly what I need," says John, whipping out his digi-cam. "I've been looking for a location like this all week."

John is a telly producer. Joan is a telly producer too. Our other Joan is a graphics designer. Of the eight people in our 'learning set' only two work in radio and I am the only one from World Service. Our facilitator/therapist is a gentle man called Dominic. He introduces himself and forms us into a circle.

"Anyone want to start?"

We look out of the windows. We pour ourselves more coffee. In the end, I do the decent thing and blurt out something I remember from Ashridge.

"Our very last session, if you remember, was a feedback session. We had to jot down one or two words on a Post-It note about our fellow course members. When I collected the Post-Its that had been written about me they all said the same thing: 'funny'; 'funny'; 'sense of humour'; 'fun'; 'a laugh'; 'candid'. Like that. I felt quite upset."

"But you are funny," says one of the Joans. "Sometimes."

"Can I just come in here," says Dominic.

He can hardly believe his luck.

"We are not here to reassure Chris or to help him feel good about himself. If he is feeling upset, *let him feel upset*. That is why we are here – to feel whatever we need to feel, and as a group to respect that. Chris, what are you feeling right now?"

"I am feeling pretty sorry for myself."

"Why is that?"

"Because I am too old to go back."

Free therapy. I am feeling what I'm feeling. Why shouldn't I splurge? Barry, who is deaf, speaks to us in sign language through the medium of a signer, who translates for him.

"I was promoted at 48. It's never too late. Look at me."

"It's too late for me, Barry. I don't want to be promoted. I have got exactly the BBC career I always wanted. But if I were to die now… Well, 'Newsroom Band 10' is not what I want on my grave stone."

"What do you want on your grave stone?" asks John.

"Er. 'Writer', probably."

"Is that your fantasy? Is that what you would rather be doing?"

I am a writer. It is not a fantasy. I write every day and some of what I write gets published.

"Yeah, but what's your absolute, perfect fantasy."

In my perfect life I would have a house in France and one in England. In each house I would have a computer. On each computer I would be writing a book. When I got bored with one book, or blocked, or if I needed a rest, I would get in my car and drive to the other one.

"Chris," says John, "that is a great fantasy. Go for it."

⊢•◦•⊣

Friday, 6 February. Newsroom, Centre Desk. Mark Byford rallies the empire. The furthest-flung outposts have been wired in to hear him being interviewed on the ringmain. Every telly monitor in the Newsroom is showing us Mark on a sofa alongside the pixie-like woman presenter of BBC1's *Breakfast Show*. Mark is well over six feet tall so he has hunched himself up out of courtesy. He's wearing a determinedly blank look on his face. Apparently, the folk at Telly Centre call him Max Bygraves, the same as we did when he first arrived at Bush House. As I enter Tithers' glass office for the 1200 Newsroom editorial meeting something becomes suddenly un-plugged and a blast of ringmain blares out loud and clear.

"We have made mistakes … We will learn from our mistakes … We must move forward …"

Mark's message isn't getting through. Or if it is, no one wants to hear it.

"We have made mistakes … It is time to move forward …"

No one understands why he is sticking so doggedly to last week's script. As the public voice of the post-Dyke BBC Mark Byford is not doing well. I am struck by an appalling thought. The Governors could well make him Director-General on the grounds that a loyal parrot is exactly what the BBC needs after being shat on by a preening budgie.

⊢•◦•⊣

Saturday, 7 February. Newsroom, Centre Desk. Someone brings a piece of classic 'Make it Happen' to my attention. We cannot quite decide if it's real.

><><>O<><<

'Post-Hutton Q & A guide sheet for managers …
Second edition …

What changes will there be now Greg's gone? Greg wouldn't have wanted us to stop anything and Mark and the rest of ExCo are absolutely committed to making sure that the progress we've made as an organisation over the last four years doesn't stop either …

Greg's focus was very much on creativity. In the light of events, will our priority focus instead shift to rebuilding our reputation as a news organisation? No … Our vision remains to be the most creative organisation in the world … Mark's phrase on this is "creativity is the flywheel of the organisation" …

Greg made 'Making it Happen' very much his own – so will it have the same drive now? Yes it will … It's Greg's legacy that we have made fantastic progress, rooted in the Values, as a result of 'Making it Happen' …

Greg made the place fun – he made everything seem possible. What will happen now? This is another part of the legacy Greg has left us. Greg's key message that "WE are the BBC" means it's up to every one of us to take responsibility and make it happen. That absolutely includes having fun. Nobody is going to stop us doing that just because Greg's gone …

But Greg was so colourful and now everything feels grey again. The men in grey suits will be back soon. No they won't … Greg has left us realising we can take the initiative to brighten our work lives up ourselves …

Did the Governors betray Greg by accepting his resignation? That's not a question we can answer … Accepting or rejecting Greg's resignation was a matter for them alone. Moving forward, it just doesn't make sense to dwell on it.

But people feel so strongly about this one … Understood, and there is a real need for people to express this emotion before we can move on … Questioning the circumstances around Greg's departure will achieve nothing. Greg would not want us to do it either … He would want us very much to concentrate on taking his legacy forward and making it real …'

＞＋◆－○－◆＋＜

Is this for real or is it a clever piece of fakery? That's always been the problem with 'Make It Happen' – the suspicion that perhaps it was simply one of Greg's gags that span hopelessly out of control, cor blimey, know what I mean?

＞＋◆－○－◆＋＜

Tuesday, 10 February. Broadcasting House, London W1. The canteen. The big hole where much of Egton House used to stand is now so vast that the whole of All Souls Church next door could be buried inside it. And there's a funny-looking crane in the middle of the site that's either sucking out mud or pumping in concrete, perhaps both. The banana and butterscotch pudding is delicious. Someone has e-mailed me an advert for a job with the United Nations in Vienna; I spend the rest of the afternoon re-working my *c.v.* with a view to applying for it.

▸━◈━◦━◈━◂

Thursday, 12 February. Newsroom, Centre Desk. Early shift, 0730 start. The things I hate most about earlies, as I never tire of reminding my colleagues, are: 1) inheriting a lead story that is wrong; 2) inheriting a lead story that is so old it's beginning to attract the flies. Today's inherited lead story reports a breakthrough in the cloning of embryos, whatever that means. It is new enough (0500) and there's nothing obviously wrong with it but the problem is I don't understand a word of it. Fortunately, an Iraq story arrives. A UN envoy, Lakhdar Brahimi, is meeting the Grand Ayatollah Sistani for crucial talks about something or other. I seize on that and drop the clones to number two. While this is going on Tithers installs himself in a spare seat on Centre Desk and starts to read-in. I hear him talking about something in one of the papers but don't pay attention until I hear him mention Andrew Gilligan's name.

"What?"

"It says here," says Tithers, "that he's joining *The Spectator* as Defence correspondent."

"They're probably hoping for the first bite at his memoirs."
"He's probably a bit young for memoirs. How old do you have to be for your memoirs?"

So far I have kept my head down during the conversation, putting Lakhdar Brahimi and the Grand Ayatollah Sistani in their place.

"Chris," says Tithers, " is it true you've been writing a diary about the BBC for the last 30 years?"

My ears prick up like a startled hare's.

"'Day one of shift pattern'," says Tithers, composing his imaginary diary out loud, " 'only three more to go. Titherington's making a nuisance of himself. Again. Decide to lead with the latest on Asian bird flu. Again.'"

He is being funny. He is aiming his whimsy not at me but at Centre Desk's other Chris, our Duty Editor, CJT, Chris Tye, who is due to retire this year after decades of loyal service to the Newsroom. Ha ha. Good old Tith.

"Excuse me, ladies," I say, "but some of us are trying to work around here."

‹—›•‹—›•‹—›

Friday, 13 February. Conference Room, Third Floor, South East Wing, Bush House. An Exco personage called Caroline Thomson has been sent over to feel our pain so she can report back on how World Service is coping without Greg Dyke. A random sample of WSNCA Band 10s has been mustered to supply her with the necessary feedback.

AG kicks off by asking Caroline how the top bosses prepared for the worst that Lord Hutton could have said in his report – because it doesn't feel as if they prepared for it at all. She replies that Hutton's remarks about the BBC were at the "extreme range" of what had been anticipated. What took the leadership aback, she says, was the fact that Lord Hutton didn't say anything at all critical about the government.

"We were expecting a sort of nil-nil draw, or perhaps a 1-1 draw. We weren't expecting a 5-nil thrashing."

"Who's 'we'?" I ask.

"The team around Greg, the lawyers, the press people, members of Exco. There were people putting the BBC's defence together."

Jeremy Skeet says the apology offered to the government on behalf of the BBC by the Vice-Chairman, Richard Ryder, on the day after Dyke's departure – the now-notorious unreserved apology – is seen by most staff as an abject cave-in. I back this up by suggesting that Mark Byford's performance to date – apologising to all and sundry every time he stands up in public – is making things worse. Liliane Landor and Andy Whitehead ask about the 'due process' investigation that Mark Byford is carrying out into how BBC News managed to get into this mess – and will anyone be sacked? Bill Rogers replies to this. He says there's a feeling that "these guys have done nothing wrong and they shouldn't be made to go", by whom he seems to mean Richard Sambrook, Stephen Mitchell and the *Today* programme's editor, Kevin Marsh.

Richard and Kevin are unknown quantities to most of us but Stephen Mitchell has been a regular visitor over the years and he does engage our sympathy. He gets most of his information about us from Mary & Co. but he has always come across as fair minded and very loyal to BBC News. But if it was "honourable" (Thomson's word) for Greg Dyke to resign why not those who were more directly involved in the dodgy dossier affair?

Bill Rogers says Mark Byford should be seen to be doing much more to support BBC News. Bill says he went to a meeting of senior managers from across the BBC and Byford virtually ignored Richard Sambrook throughout, with the result that "he was as near to tears as I have ever seen him." Tithers says the last time he was at Telly Centre he bumped into Kevin Marsh "and he looked like he was going through hell." Caroline Thomson says she thinks the next Chairman of Governors will be an old-style Tory grandee, maybe Douglas Hurd, and that the next D-G will be someone with extensive experience of public broadcasting, "and it will not be me because I am not applying."

It seems not to have occurred to Caroline that Greg Dyke's downfall does not overly vex us at World Service. According to Lord Hutton, it is BBC News who messed up so they should take the rap. Greg's exit has hardly been mentioned in the Newsroom Log. The single entry that's provoked the most heat in Talkback so far this year concerns the proper pronunciation of the word covert.

'You wouldn't say "I coe-vered my face would you? So why say coe-vert. It's nonsensical to do so. Please stop it or I will explode.'

⊱⋅•⋅⊰

Saturday, 14 February. Newsroom, Centre Desk. At 1000 hours GMT today we make history. For the first time ever there are 11 items in the BBC World Service Central Core:

STORY SLUG	DURATION (in seconds)
CEN 1000 TOP	20
CEN 1000 FALLUJAH ATTACK	38

CEN 0930 IRAQ NEIGHBOURS	23
CEN 1000 US TV ARAB	20
CEN 0930 BUSH WAR RECORD	34
CEN 1000 AFGHAN GUANTANAMO	32
CEN 0100 AFRICAN FOOTBALL	28
CEN 1000 S KOREA SUMO	25
CEN 0900 INDIA PAKISTAN CRICKET	21
CEN 0530 CHINA EXECUTION	24
CEN 0300 JAPAN YACHTSMAN	27

I bet Richard Sambrook wishes he was back in charge of a news bulletin right now. Not only is he going through hell in the form of a disciplinary process but he also has to keep churning out routine managerial bilge. He's sent us an email about that staff survey we had to complete last year. While there are positive scores in some areas – according to the figures, 81 per cent of us feel BBC News is an exciting place to work – there is huge scope for improvement in others – only 29 per cent of staff think their managers deal with poor performance effectively. Richard says his 'Making it Happen' strategy will have to be re-focused in order to address the areas where progress needs to be made – like the *Today* programme perhaps.

━━━◦━━━

Sunday, 15 February. Newsroom, Centre Desk. Slow shifts remind us all over again how much of our stock in trade is to do with the re-packaging of sudden death as a commodity. As I head off for my lunch break half of the Central Core is made up of disasters.

CEN 1130 CHINA FIRE More than 50 people perish in a fire in a shopping complex

CEN 1130 UGANDA ACCIDENT 26 people burn to death after a mini bus crashes into a fuel truck

CEN 1130 RUSSIA COLLAPSE At least 25 die after a roof collapses onto a swimming pool

CEN 0730 PAKISTAN QUAKE Two earthquakes leave at least 18 dead

EUR 1300 BRITAIN RAIL ACCIDENT Runaway rail truck kills four.

I have hardly come back from the Charing Cross Road when reports started coming in of another fire in China: 39 people killed in a temple. I ask SMJ to update the 1130 story and before he's finished it the following news comes in on the wires:

1437 INDIA DROWNINGS Boat capsizes, River Ganges, Varanasi – 17 dead.

1450 SCOTTISH CRASH Car driver loses control, Glenrothes, Fife – 3 dead.

1450 BODY FOUND Chinese cockle picker washed up in Morecambe Bay, Lancs – 1 dead.

1458 NEPAL KILLING Head of Nepal's Maoist Victims Association assassinated in Kathmandu – 1 dead.

>―•―○―•―<

Saturday, 21 February. Newsroom, Centre Desk. Another night shift soured by wrangling with Newsgathering. Tithers has asked us to collect examples of World Service receiving short measure so this time I put my gripes in writing.

'Firstly, Bangkok was asked to file for the 0500 bulletin but didn't file until 0502. In chat it emerged that the correspondent was grumpy because he didn't think the story (bird flu kills cat in Thailand) warranted a piece, in which case he should have argued his case at the outset ... Secondly, we were offered a two-way with a correspondent about Guantanamo Bay for the 0400 and the Reel dropped another piece to make room for it but the correspondent failed to show; reports say he was heard talking to Radio Five Live instead ... A third correspondent was booked in good time as the comeback piece on Iran elections for the 0500 and she too went to Five Live but failed to show for us. Intake said she was on standby for a call from the studio that never came. All in all a typical night shift. And so home to bed ...'

>―•―○―•―<

Monday, 23 February. Newsroom, Centre Desk. Any more night shifts like this and I could well become the first SDE on Centre Desk to combust spontaneously. At 0603 hours, at the end of our last, long shift before our well-earned days off, AFP flashes a snap about a bomb going off in Kirkuk, in northern Iraq, just in time to give us a shiny new lead to hand over to the incoming early shift. RD prepares our snap and Reuters comes up within minutes as the second source.

We green the snap and about two minutes later, much to our surprise, the Traffic tannoy announces that Stephen Sackur is on the line – *in Kirkuk!* He is standing outside the bombed police headquarters, surrounded by smoking debris and scorched body parts. A BBC correspondent is standing at the epicentre of world news right now and CNN doesn't even have a map to put on screen! Sackur does his generic minute like every good correspondent should and RD uses it to storify* his snap with plenty of colour.

In the meantime our Intake editor has received a call from the Newsgathering editor at Telly Centre. Newsgathering has done exactly the right thing and put Sackur straight through to World Service for a two-way but the folk on the Third Floor aren't picking up the line.

"What?"

"The *World Today* isn't picking up."

"What are they doing?"

The Intake editor turns up the audio feed on her desk so we can hear *The World Today* programme. The newsreader is reading the two-minute summary at 0630.

"Oh," says Intake, "they'll be taking him after the summary. There's been a bit of a problem with Sackur's connection. He's on his mobile."

The summary ends. *The World Today* presenter launches into

a cue about the imminent expansion of the European Union to include new member states. *The World Today* is first in the queue for a Stephen Sackur scoop and they haven't taken him. No one knows why. The Intake editor is beside herself. I run down to the Third Floor three steps at a time and barge into the *World Today* office. *The World Today* editor is on the phone.

"What's going on? We've got a scoop on our hands, CNN is nowhere and your presenter's chatting away about the European Union. Why haven't you taken Sackur?"

The *World Today* editor doesn't know what I'm talking about. But someone on his programme must know because the Intake desk has told News Traffic to switch Stephen Sackur though to S38 *and he's hanging on the line*!

"Oh," he says.

I stamp down the corridor to studio S38. Too late. Sackur has gone. News Traffic have taken the line back.

"Argh!"

I address myself to *The World Today* studio producer.

"What do you think BBC Newsgathering thinks of us when they give us a scoop and we can't take it? What do you think Stephen Sackur thinks of the World Service right now?"

"Chris, we lost the line."

"And then you got it back again."

"We lost that one too. He kept dropping out."

It is neither the time nor the place. Throwing a tantrum in a radio studio while a programme is on air is the very height of bad manners, in fact it's a crime.

"I don't know why we bother!"

When I get back to my seat in the Newsroom I notice that my right leg is shaking. Normally, the Monday morning that ends a run of night shifts is a very happy moment – the start of a whole week of off days. Today it is a complete pisser.

Handling news requires intelligence, general knowledge, dexterity with language, a decisive approach to risk and a reliable scepticism in assessing the world's wicked ways. Doing that for ten hours a night for four consecutive nights demands mental and physical resilience. All that is required of Current Affairs producers, if the Newsroom has done its job properly, is to pick up a phone, ask some pundit to share their opinions about what's in the news and then get someone else to switch them through to the right studio. A blindfold monkey could do it with the right kind of on-the-job training.

The first mistake was to merge World Service News with World Service Current Affairs to save money. The second big mistake was to put Current Affairs editors in charge of WSNCA with a free hand to rethink the possibilities. Those two strategic blunders did our listeners no favours at all.

><><><>

FROM: Bill Rogers.
SENT: 2 March 2004.
TO: Band 10s.
SUBJECT: Inconvenient.

'The work to refurbish our toilets in SE wing has been disrupted by a serious flood, requiring repairs to most of the ladies toilets. So LST has taken the following action. The third, fifth and seventh floor gents are still for gentlemen only. The fourth and the sixth floor gents toilets have been re-designated as ladies toilets until further notice. The LG toilets are operating as they always have – ladies please use ladies, gents please use gents. We apologise for the inconvenience! Bill Rogers, Managing Editor, Radio News.'

CHAPTER TWELVE

No Guru, No Method

Friday, 5 March. White City. Action Learning Set. We are back in the wedge shaped room overlooking the A4 flyover. I was wrong about our facilitator/therapist's name; it is Hugh not Dominic. He used to be an actor. He says the first time he was told he would be performing without a prompter, he felt nervous. Then he discovered *it was liberating!*

Barry turns up with a new signer. They both leave early because of a crisis back in the office. John mooches in late with bags under his eyes, sipping a Starbuck's Frappuccino. He and one of the Joans supply the group dynamic. John unburdens himself of a crisis he's having with some researcher in the office while Joan makes practical suggestions. When it comes to telly producers and their tantrums she's been there, done that. I find the whole thing very relaxing, sipping coffee and engaging in active listening until Hugh calls time.

<hr/>

Sunday, 7 March. Newsroom, Centre Desk. The big news is that the acting-Editor, Bill Rogers, has returned whence he came and posted his last note in Log Advisory.

'I've promised a range of people I'll keep turning up at Bush whether you like it or not,' he writes. 'We still have stuff to do. Both Steve Mitchell and Richard Sambrook want to come and talk to you, when their diaries permit. I've promised Nigel and others that we'll debate the "embeds" report with Mark Damazer ere long. Once again, it's been a pleasure to work with the civilising influence of the Bush editorial team … I look forward to seeing you all in relaxed circumstances at Bush, TVC – and the Elysian Fields of New BH, should we last that long ... You're in good hands with Liliane and Steve T.'

Bill has been a much more friendly, newsy and hands-off type of Telly Centre interloper than some we've had foisted on us. He was also good at jokes. But it's always a relief to see the back of them.

><+>—O—<+>—<

Monday, 8 March. Home, London SW4. Off sick, under the duvet. I listen to a run of World Service news bulletins: Iraq; Iran; the Greek election. None of it sounds in any way interesting or relevant to someone with a raging sore throat and thick head.

><+>—O—<+>—<

Thursday, 18 March. Newsroom, Centre Desk. Night shift. Interesting chat with the ladies on the Intake desk about how we might attract more women to work on news bulletins. Afterwards, MAC sends me an action plan based on her deep and wide understanding of female psychology.

'Strategy to attract more women to Centre Desk.

- More fluffy stuff around the place, eg. kittens.

- More cakes.

- More pink furniture.

- Marks & Spencer's vouchers for all women on Centre Desk.

- Love songs on the News Traffic tannoy instead of boring old news correspondents.'

Tuesday, 30 March. To Haverstock Hill on a clear, bright Spring day. I almost make myself late on account of the spadework I'm doing on the new patio. I have laid bare the tangled roots of the bay tree and a couple of the thicker ones are giving real trouble. Unusually, Alan speaks first.

"Welcome to the last therapy session."

"Yeah."

I lie on the couch and shut my eyes. Someone in the flat upstairs is using a power drill, filling Alan's room with literal vibrations. I lie still with my eyes closed. Eventually, the image of the stranded baby appears. For the past three years, whenever I have come to Haverstock Hill with nothing particularly urgent to say, the baby in need has appeared, sitting on the ground in his nappy, looking up at me over his shoulder. This time, for the first time, I pick him up.

"It sounds rather too neat," I suggest.

Today, for the first time, I pick up the baby when he holds up his arms beseechingly. I pick him up, give him some attention, settle him on my hip and carry him off.

"It's too neat, too neat."

"What happens, happens," says Alan. "Don't let that cynical journalist get in the way."

My last therapy session ends there and then with 40 minutes left on the clock. I lie still for a while longer, soaking up the Haverstock Hill vibes for old times' sake. I can't take them with me. I can't come back. I seem to be feeling okay about that.

More drilling. More banging. More drilling. People move in, they re-wire, they paper over the cracks, they move on. That's Haverstock Hill.

"Underpin and make good," says Alan. "When I first moved to Hampstead there were a couple of jobbing builders around here who called themselves 'Underpin & Makegood'. I used to like seeing their van. I thought it was a good analogy for therapy."

"We're at time now, Alan," I say. "That's the last session over."

That makes him laugh, me stealing his lines. He says he has enjoyed working with me. He says he's touched that I let him in. He wishes me every success. We hug like father and son and I don't feel like crying.

"Goodbye, Chris."

I know I'm never coming back.

"Goodbye, Alan, and thank you. You're a good one. You've been a good therapist for me and … I'm very grateful. Thank you."

◦──◦──◦──◦

Friday, 2 April. Newsroom, Centre Desk. Michael Grade has been appointed Chairman of the BBC Board of Governors in place of Gavyn Davies. Mark Byford is first in the queue with congratulations.

'Michael is one of the major world figures in Broadcasting and the wider creative industry, with an outstanding record of achievement … deep understanding of broadcasting … passionate about creativity … everyone in the BBC will warmly welcome this exciting appointment … It's great that Michael is coming back …'

Grade's first job, after he's got his feet under the desk, will be to head-hunt someone to be his next Director-General. I think we can safely rule out anyone currently working for the BBC.

⊳⋅⋄⋅○⋅⋄⋅⊲

Saturday 3 April. Newsroom, Centre Desk. 0730 start. The magnolia trees are in luscious full flower. One of them blooms at the start of my bike ride, two of them greet me at the end of it – one each side of the iron gates of St. Mary-le-Strand church. While I am logging on to ENPS, someone shows me a fantastic photo of Mark Byford in *The Guardian*. There was a ceremony yesterday to welcome Michael Grade back to the BBC and Mark had to introduce him. The photo shows Michael Grade walking onto to the set with a big smile and his arm outstretched to shake hands but Mark has already turned away with a clenched frown, mouth set, head down, shoulders hunched – looking like some sort of deputy stand-in who's just failed to fill the moment.

The verdict on Byford is set in stone but Centre Desk is prepared to give Michael Grade the benefit of the doubt, for the time being, because the Governors could have chosen someone much worse. It was Grade who first started dumbing down Channel Four when he was in charge there, although when I mention the shows he mentored, like *The Word* and *The Girlie Show*, no one else remembers them. Or does that prove my point?

The *Newshour* editor arrives from the Third Floor to see what we might have in mind for the morning's news. The lead story is about the United States warning people on public transport to be vigilant against suspected bombs. The second headline is reporting early results in the Sri Lankan general election.

"Sorry," I say. "It's all looking a bit dull at the moment."

"Thanks," says the *Newshour* editor. "Let me know if you have any bright ideas."

Liliane Landor phones in from home to touch base after a dutiful listen to our 0800 bulletin. The WSNCA leadership runs a little weekend rota of its own for keeping an eye on us.

"Hello," she says, "who's that?"

"Chris Moore."

"Chris, what a pleasant surprise. What's it like?"

She means the news.

"Did you hear it?"

"I did."

"You know you're in a bad way, Liliane, when Sri Lanka is poised to be the next lead story. But don't worry. We're working on something."

"What are you working on?"

The only thing I know for sure that we are working on is something about old-age pensioners holding a protest march in Rome. I can't use that as my secret weapon.

"One or two Euro things that haven't quite gelled yet. Relax. Go to Sainsbury's. Have a day off. Have a cappuccino. The sun is shining. Do what people do on a Saturday when Spring is in the air."

Now that Bill Rogers has departed, Liliane is in charge, which is probably why she feels obliged to take more than her usual interest in what the Newsroom is doing. After a few more weekends she will get the hang of things. The rule for touching base at weekends is to keep it chatty and hang up quick.

"Bye-ee!"

At 0854 Reuters snaps a quote from the Burmese foreign minister saying that the pro-democracy leader, Aung San Suu Kyi, is going to be released soon from house arrest. At 0902 the AP wire comes up with the same quote. The source is a television interview recorded by the Japanese broadcaster, NHK. Our snap just makes it into the 0900 bulletin. At 0920 Liliane phones in again. Doesn't she *want* to be out in the sunshine?

"I just had Phil Harding on the phone," she says. "He heard the snap at the end of the bulletin. Do you think we should be mounting some kind of special?"

A special edition of *World Briefing*? Phil Harding must be out of his mind.

"But it's Aung San Suu Kyi," says Liliane. "She's a big name."

"Hold on," I say. "We haven't got a correspondent's despatch yet. Intake has only just set the Bangkok bureau on the case. You know what the Burmese are like. This story has got deniability written all over it."

"What do you mean, deniability?"

"This foreign minister – he is just one guy from the junta, right? He lands at Bangkok; he walks into a posse of hacks throwing questions at him about Aung San Suu Kyi; he's not media savvy; he says the first thing that comes into his head and jumps in the car and drives off. As soon as this gets back to Rangoon, they'll deny it. The Burmese *hate* making news."

"So did he say it or not?"

"He said something. We've got RTR and AP with the same quote. Kylie's checking it out and will file a despatch. But so what – it's a Burma story."

"So no special?"

"If Aung San Suu Kyi walks out of her compound and makes a speech we can think again. But at the moment all we've got is an OK lead story for a slow Saturday. Let's wait and see."

"Alright. I'll tell him that."

About ten minutes later, Kylie Morris files her despatch from Bangkok. It is a straightforward re-write of the agency stuff, short and to the point. We all cheer up. They're happy on Third Floor. We're happy in the Newsroom. We have a new lead story for the top of the bulletin and a needle match between Arsenal and Man United to look forward to, plus the Grand National, for which we are organising a sweepstake.

At about 1020 the *Newshour* editor arrives from downstairs, talking into her mobile phone.

"He's not plugged in," she's saying, "that's what the problem is, he's not plugged in."

Somehow I have managed to kick my phone plug out of the electronic box of tricks under my desk. It happens about once per shift. The *Newshour* editor hands me her mobile.

"It's Liliane," she says, "she's been trying to get you."

Phil Harding has been on the phone again. He doesn't see Burma as just another OK lead story for a slow Saturday. And he says he's confused that he didn't hear anything about deniability in our 1000 bulletin. I make a sound like '*fffttt!*' This is exactly what happens when the news get caught in a tangle between bosses. At weekends they should all just unplug their phones and leave us alone to get on with it. I try explaining again to Liliane my reservations about going large on the Burma story. The Intake editor butts in while I'm talking. She's got Kylie on the line. I put Liliane on hold.

"Kylie?"

"Hi, Chris. AFP have just got onto the Burma story and they say it's not true."

"How do you mean?"

"They say there's been a translation error."

"Great."

"Yeah. AFP are saying that NHK aren't running the story even though they did the original interview."

"Liliane, can you hear any of this ...?"

"What?"

I'm standing at the Intake desk with a phone pressed to each ear.

"Kylie," I tell Liliane, "says the story's bollocks."

Kylie can hear me on the other phone.

"I'm not saying it's bollocks," she says, "it's just that we're going to have to row back."

"What?" says Liliane, in my other ear. "What's going on, Chris?"

I explain the problem to her. That highly deniable Burma story that Phil Harding thought might possibly be a rolling news event of global significance has been denied even before it's got back to Rangoon.

"Okay," says Liliane. "So what are we going to do?"

It is the weekend. Spring has arrived and the sun is shining.

"You are on a day off. I am on shift. So I suggest you go and buy an ice cream, or whatever, while I sit here and sort out Burma. Go on. Have a day off on your day off!"

Kylie and I agree a form of words to start us backtracking on our existing story and she goes off to re-write her despatch. At 1100 World Service news goes on air with a headline saying that remarks from the Burmese foreign minister have led to suggestions that the Burmese pro-democracy leader, Aung San Suu Kyi, might be released soon from house arrest – but no one is holding their breath. And the search has begun for a better lead story. In the meantime, in the Newsroom, the Band 10 on Centre Desk has had enough of this shift already and is taking an early lunch break in the Charing Cross Road in order to get back in time for the footie and the biggest horse race of the year.

>-+-+-0-+-+-<

Wednesday, 21 April. Save the Children charity shop, Clapham High Street, SW9. Trawling the bookshelves I come across *John P. Kotter On What Leaders Really Do* by John P. Kotter. That's Kotter with a K, the visionary business guru mentioned by Greg Dyke in his speech at Ashridge. Kotter is the man who inspired Greg to launch 'Make it Happen'.

> 'Although change generally involves a complex multistage process, regardless of setting, some essential actions taken by effective managers with transformational goals always vary from case to case to fit key contingencies in their situations. An insensitivity to local contingencies ... can produce disaster.'

Almost every Kotter sentence needs to be read twice.

> 'What a manager/leader does on a minute-by-minute, hour-by-hour basis rarely fits any stereotype of manager, heroic leader, or executive, a fact that can create considerable confusion for those in managerial jobs, especially newcomers. Daily observable behaviour is nevertheless understandable if one takes into consideration the diverse tasks (including both leadership and management), the difficult work (including both maintenance and change), and the web of relationships (which goes far beyond formal hierarchy) that come with the territory ...'

Each Kotter paragraph leaves me feeling ... confused. But might the book be worth its price, just to be able to quote from it next time I go to Ashridge? I turn to the front of the book for the first time to check the price. Inside the front cover is an inscription written with a felt tip pen in a thick, backward-slanted hand.

'To Nigel. Thank you for helping to "make it happen" [signed] Greg'.

⊢•◆•○•◆•⊣

Monday, 26 April. White City, Action Learning Set. We're in the Bob Dylan room this time because the wedge-shaped, glass-walled space named after Jimi Hendrix is unavailable. John has already arrived and is dealing with a big sandwich while chomping out instructions on his mobile phone.

"John," I say, "let go, mate. You're not here to work. Leave it."

The hospitality appears not to have been ordered so I schlep down to the designer sandwich boutique on the ground floor for a ham and salad baguette, the price of which makes me feel grumpy. Plus, we are missing three people – Simone and the two Joans. Eventually, the big telly Joan trolls in saying she got lost on the way. Hugh explains that the Scottish Joan is ill and Simone had a prior commitment. So eventually, about 1330, we get down to it, with John opening the bidding.

He lay awake most of last night, worrying about work. He nodded off about four, woke up at six and came into the office to write scripts. John says he hardly ever gets a full night's kip. He's got into the habit of lying awake at night figuring out how to defend himself against potential lawsuits. As a result, he has never lost a lawsuit and is now an expert at contingency planning. Which is good at one level because it means he is usually able to fix stuff that goes wrong. But it's bad at the personal level because of the permanent lack of sleep which is why he looks so wrecked all the time.

"I have this basic fear that I will be found out, that I am not good enough. What worries me is the thought that someone is going to point to one of my programmes and say 'that's shit, you're crap' and I won't have a word to say in my defence."

If my theory about John is correct he knows what his problem is.

"Perhaps nobody told you, John, or perhaps they did but you didn't hear it – you were always good enough."

It is me speaking, old clever clogs, the ex-therapee. I want John to hear something in case he has never heard it from anyone else.

"Young John always tried his best, didn't he? He was always lovable. But somehow, along the way, you have learned to suspect yourself. The people who taught you that were wrong. That is an objective fact. You were always good enough and you still are. You are good enough for all the people in this room. That's the problem with the BBC. We are all good enough but some of us can't quite believe it."

―――○―――

Friday, 30 April. Kettner's Restaurant and Champagne Bar, Romilly Street, Soho, London W1. WSNCA Band 10 Awayday. Acting Editor, Liliane Landor, is in the chair. We're in a somewhat dingy upstairs room with a good view through the open window of the pastry cooks at work over the road in Patisserie Bertaux, established 1851. Lunch turns out to be the cheapest option offered on the corporate menu: garlic mushrooms; pizza or lasagne; chocolate mousse or apple pie. Liliane's laxity as chairperson means that we don't start eating until 1330, by which stage we are all ravenously hungry.

The insider gossip over lunch says that Mark Byford remains favourite to be the next Director-General (shock, horror) because of his perceived loyalty to the Governors. The rest of the BBC Executive is said to despair of him as an interloper from Bush House (!) but no one has yet come forward to run against him. Apparently, Mark Thompson's wife doesn't want him to go for the job because of the stress. Michael Jackson is said to be reluctant. And Jenny 'Too Old' Abramsky is considered to be definitely too Radio if not actually too old.

The problem is seen to be this: Mark Byford gets good press. That's because he's the corporate face of World Service and the Governors get their information about the BBC from reading the papers not from meeting BBC staff. The Governors, as representatives of the British taxpayer, cling to the notion that Bush House represents a beacon of integrity in our murky old world. They appear to think that Mark Byford might be able to sprinkle some World Service magic dust to help restore credibility. 'Trust' and 'reliability' are enjoying a post-Hutton vogue in the official vocabulary.

⊷•○•⊷

Saturday, 1 May. Newsroom, Centre Desk. First of four night shifts. As always, the first thing Centre Desk wants to know after we have got the first bulletin out of the way is what was discussed at the Awayday.

"Impartiality."

"What about it?"

"Liliane seemingly wants less of it. Under certain circumstances."

After lunch at Kettner's yesterday we spent the afternoon listening to assorted clips of BBC interviewers being biased. One excerpt featured a spokesman for the British National Party (BNP), being interrogated in a thoroughly aggressive manner. SAT said that after listening to it that she felt quite sorry for the guy because of the interviewer's blatant hostility.

"Yes," said Liliane, "and that's the last thing we want. There's no point having the BNP on the show if they're going to come out of it looking good."

It seems to be the British bit of the British Broadcasting Corporation that she doesn't quite get – the idea that the job is *always* to report the news with detachment whether it suits us or not. Without that we are just one more partial source in an ever expanding universe of noise, babblement and propaganda.

Greg Dyke has gone. 'Make it Happen' must surely follow. But things won't get better all at once and they could get worse. Lord Hutton's inquiry has tarnished the reputation of BBC News to which World Service is yoked like two oxen of unequal power and pedigree. Inside Bush House we are pulling our weight but the road ahead is veiled in doubt and jeopardy. The sunlit uplands we were promised at the start of the journey remain as distant as ever.

BBC WORLD SERVICE
NEWSROOM GLOSSARY

Actuality. The real thing, any radio or television recording of an actual event, usually a news conference, speech or interview. From the French, *actualite*.

Airlock. The door into the Newsroom from the Fourth Flour landing of South East Wing led into a sort of vestibule from which another door opened into the Newsroom proper. This vestibule with its deep window recess was a convenient space for private conversations out of sight and earshot of inquisitive colleagues, having previously been a popular venue for cigarette smokers.

Ariel. The BBC staff newspaper, named after the sprite in Shakespeare's play, *The Tempest*. *Ariel's* slavish loyalty to the pro-management line earned it the nickname, *Pravda*, after the organ of the Russian Communist Party.

Autograph book. A BBC retirement gift in the form of an album bound in *faux* leather and embossed in gilt with the retiring person's name. Autograph books were kept in the **SDE's drawer** and smuggled from desk to desk in the weeks before retirement, allowing colleagues to pay tribute in scribbled valedictions to the near departed.

BBC Club. In every major BBC building there was a branch of the BBC Club with a bar. The Club in Bush House was in the window-less basement next to the canteen. One entire wall was taken up by a row of aquaria containing tropical fish.

BECTU. The Broadcasting, Entertainment, Cinematograph and Technicians' Union, one of the two main unions recognised within the BBC alongside the **NUJ.** BBC bosses were always keen to exploit differences between the two to prevent agreement on joint action.

Billboard. The menu at the opening of a Current Affairs programme telling the listener what's in store. In the World Service it always ended with the phrase, "but first a bulletin of world news …"

Black line, black bar. When a programme **running order** was assembled in **ENPS** the black line on the screen indicated the end of the programme. Any items listed 'below the line' were there to await confirmation, or to be used to fill time in the event of plans going awry 'above the line' before or during transmission.

Boil. To boil a story was to shrink it in size to make room for another item in the bulletin. Hence, "Can you boil the French President down to twenty seconds please."

Brackets. Sentences, or parts of sentences, were written in (brackets) to indicate to a newsreader or translator that they were optional. When a sentence was put in brackets the **ENPS** system didn't count it as part of the timed **length** of the story.

Cans. Headphones. Each desk in the Newsroom was provided with cans which could be plugged into the **ringmain** carrying live feeds of BBC programmes and **News Traffic**.

Centre Block. The place in Bush House where the senior leadership had their offices. As in, "Heard the latest wheeze from Centre Block?"

Clip. To 'clip' a piece of audio was to extract a sound-bite from it. See also, **Grab**.

Copy. Journalists' jargon for news on paper.

Copytaste. To scan lots of copy quickly with a view to identifying the news in it.

Copytaster. A journalist specifically employed to copytaste all day. Once upon a time in the Newsroom there were two of them working side by side simultaneously; by the time Greg Dyke had gone there was none.

Core, Core News. The Central Core was a list of up-to-date stories maintained by Centre Desk from which actual news bulletins were compiled.

Corrected version. When an error came to light in a news story it always had to be corrected. But see also, **Literal** and **Silent fix**.

Dark side. Every Newsroom team inherited its bulletin from one team and handed it on to another, relay style. Every journalist on the rota therefore met colleagues from two other teams every day. There were six teams in the Newsroom altogether and those three teams that were never seen in person, except at Awaydays, were known as the Dark Side.

Dawns. The correct word for night shifts in Bush House. Origin obscure.

Drop. To drop something was to print it. As in, "Can you drop me a copy of the 0900 Top, please – my printer's jammed."

Downstairs. The **Third Floor**, as seen from the Newsroom.

ENPS. Electronic News Production System. The all-powerful computer software deployed across the BBC News for generating news items, programmes and bulletins in the form of story templates and programme grids.

F.C.O. The Foreign & Commonwealth Office, the government department responsible for funding the BBC World Service and for exercising oversight on behalf of Parliament. Ultimately, it was to prove perfidious.

F.O.C. Father of Chapel – the NUJ shop steward in any BBC newsroom. In the case of a woman, Mother of Chapel.

Fourth Floor. The generic term for the Newsroom and its programmes, including news bulletins, *World Briefing* and *From Our Own Correspondent* when that was moved there.

Grab. A hated noun and verb. It referred to the action of 'grabbing' a piece of audio from the telly and turning it into a radio sound-bite. It was a finicky procedure and very often sounded horrible on air. However, as successive rounds of budget cuts bit deeper and deeper, 'grabs' were increasingly the only source of **actuality**.

Handover, hand over. The period at the intersection of two Newsroom shifts during the 24-hour cycle, the moment when responsibility for Centre Desk and its news changed hands and an important marker in the day's routine. Also, an opportunity to exchange gossip, speculation and recrimination. Certain protocols were observed. It was very bad form, for example, to turn up late and miss 'the handover'.

Green. Every story template in **ENPS** had a check box. No story could be broadcast while the box remained red; it could only be transmitted once an editor had 'greened' it.

Herogram. A generic e-mail from an exalted BBC personage couched in congratulatory terms and distributed wholesale after any conspicuous achievement. A much derided form of 'internal communication'.

Hold. To put a 'hold' on a story was to question its veracity in whole or in part and to stop it being broadcast until doubts could be clarified. See also, **Kill.**

Hours. All times in Bush House were given in the 24-hour clock. Thus, 'the 0500' meant the bulletin broadcast at five o'clock in the morning, Greenwich Mean Time.

House style. The rules specifying English usage in WSNCA, as spelled out in the Style Book. More followed in the breach than the observance, particularly on the **Third Floor**.

Human Resources. Greg Dyke's preferred term for Personnel' when he declared war on bureaucracy and created a shambles. For a considerable period the personnel functions required by Fourth Floor, South East Wing, Bush House, London WC1, were off-shored to a call centre in Belfast.

Kill. To kill a story was to stop it from being broadcast with immediate effect, usually on the grounds that it was suspected of being seriously wrong.

Knock down. The verb used when a journalist decided against a story. See also, **Spike.**

Language sections. A 'section' was the old-fashioned bureaucratic term for any of the foreign language outlets of the World Service responsible for translating the Newsroom's stories and despatches for their listeners. The biggest sections, such as Arabic, broadcast day and night and employed scores of translators. The smaller sections, such as the Sinhalas, employed barely half-a-dozen.

Length. At World Service the length of a news story or despatch was measured in minutes and seconds, calculated by **ENPS** at the rate of three words per second.

Level. A technical term for the optimum quantum of audio input required for a recording to sound professionally balanced when broadcast. To 'take level' was to adjust the sound levels to optimum while someone was talking into the microphone.

Literal. Short for 'literal error', usually a spelling mistake. It was a crime on Centre Desk to submit a story for **greening** without checking it carefully for literals but they always sneaked through. Newsreaders pounced on them with accusatory glee.

Monitoring. The BBC ran a Monitoring Service at a former stately home outside Reading where staff from foreign countries were employed to eavesdrop on other radio stations to gather news. It had an excellent canteen with a view of the grounds.

Net head. A headline of six words or less added (in brackets) to the bottom of every Newsroom story. Net heads were introduced when a substantial cadre of staff left the World Service to set up the BBC's first news service on the internet, which expanded rapidly into the entity now known as *BBC Online.*

News Traffic. The desk run by BBC **Newsgathering** as the central distribution point for reporters and correspondents filing despatches. Once a correspondent was on the line and ready to file Traffic announced the fact on the Traffic tannoy. The **SDE**'s telephone on Centre Desk was equipped with a key enabling him or her to hold a three-way conversation with Traffic and the correspondent in question. This was known as 'coming across the line', as in, "Don't go, Joe – Bush House is coming across the line.'

Newsgathering. Before the creation of Newsgathering, Television News, Radio News and World Service appointed their own reporters and foreign correspondents. The material they filed was shared freely but each correspondent answered directly to the priorities of his or her own managers and news editors. After the creation of Newsgathering, the BBC's reporters and correspondents lost their individual focus and started to look and sound like telly folk.

Newsinf. Short for News Information, the name of the Newsroom's cuttings library in the pre-digital era. Newsinf remained as a colloquial term long after all the paper files and indexes had been shipped off in a skip. 'Newsinf' as a noun meant any piece of archival source material. To 'newsinf' a story was to check it against a piece of archive.

Newsroom Log. In the pre-digital Newsroom, next to the News About Britain desk, was a wooden desk with a drawer in it. Inside was the Newsroom Log, a plastic folder for important memos about operational matters and rulings on **house style**. Each journalist was expected to check the Log as part of the **reading-in** process at the start of every shift. When computers replaced typewriters the Log became a folder in **ENPS** called **Log Advisory** which was accessible to all.

Nose. The nose of a story was it's opening sentence. To **re-nose** a story was to give it a new top line. The nose was also the organ by which a journalist identified the germ in any event that made it newsworthy.

NUJ. The National Union of Journalists. NUJ members in the BBC persisted in calling their branches 'chapels' in the style of Fleet Street newspapers (see **FOC**). NUJ membership was strong in the Bush House Newsroom and its chapel could usually be relied upon to stick up for its members' rights both collective and individual.

Off rota. When a member of Newsroom staff was required to work on some boss's pet project instead of a particular Newsroom desk it was known as 'working off rota'. This of course created a gap on the rota which needed to be 'filled'. Hence, "I haven't seen you for ages, what are you doing in today?" "Oh, I'm filling in on the Arabic desk.'

Pashto Service. The World Service **language section** employing Pashto speakers, one of the main languages of Afghanistan. Urdu was anther, the main language for broadcasting to Pakistan. Other sections identified by language included the Hausas, for Nigeria, and the Swahilis, for Kenya.

Piece. An item of news, a report, a despatch, anything made by a journalist for broadcast.

Piece to camera. A stand up shot at the beginning or end of a telly report intended to establish authenticity. In Paris, for example, the piece to camera always had to show the Eiffel Tower.

Pigeon holes. The alphabetically arranged letter racks to which pay slips and other necessary BBC communications were delivered in the Newsroom. The internal mail service made deliveries twice a day.

Producer. A journalist employed to make radio or television programmes.

Producer Guidelines. The rulebook for BBC producers.

Reading-in. The half-hour or so after the **handover** devoted to familiarising oneself with the quality and quantity of news processed by the previous shift.

Reel. *Radio Newsreel*, the first and longest-running programme produced in the Newsroom before it was replaced by *Newsdesk* and then *World Briefing*. These later re-incarnations of the programme stayed in the same area of the Newsroom because that's where the necessary under-floor wiring was situated. Some longer-serving staff carried on calling that area 'the Reel' because whatever new format was devised, and whatever the programme might be called, it was still first and foremost a programme dependent on correspondents' despatches. Calling *World Briefing* 'the Reel' sometimes annoyed its pioneers and progenitors.

Rejig. A euphemism for re-writing a factually correct story to make it sound better.

Ringmain. The audio circuit with an access point at every desk whereby any journalist could eavesdrop on BBC material being recorded or broadcast.

Rip and Read. An hourly news summary compiled by the domestic radio newsroom at Telly Centre which in its earliest days was spewed out on teleprinters all over the BBC.

Rolling thunder. An epithet for 'rolling news', the style of broadcasting which collapsed the schedule of individual programmes and replaced them with one long Current Affairs sequence. Once the **Third Floor** had established its ascendancy over the Newsroom, rolling thunder was inflicted on the listener with increasing frequency.

Row back. To row back on a story (as with oars) was to dilute its impact after the receipt of equivocal information. 'Rowing back' was the opposite of 'hardening up' a story. See also **Hold** and **Kill**.

Running order. Jargon for the sequence of recorded or live items comprising a programme or news bulletin, represented in **ENPS** in the form of a grid.

S.D.E. Senior Duty Editor. The man or woman on Centre Desk responsible for deciding the news, hour by hour, in Bush House. SDEs were paid according to Band 10 of the pay scale but carried greater responsibilities than Band 10s in other parts of BBC News.

SDE's drawer. The Newsroom repository for lost property as well as important or confidential documents - **autograph books** for retirees, folders detailing emergency procedures, the key to the stationery cupboard, etcetera.

S.P.S. Special Personal Salary.

S.M., Studio Manager. Someone employed by the BBC to manage the technical side of transmitting a radio programme, the essential human link between producers and listeners. The ideal studio manager was someone of calm temperament and nimble thinking when it came to handling the complexity of switches, buttons and dials of his or her studio control panel. Experienced SMs were held in esteem and affection in the Newsroom for saving many a programme scrambled together at the last minute.

Satfeed. The regular, routine delivery of news by satellite in the form of telly pictures.

Shot list. The breaking down of a television report into its component parts, shot by shot. Telly correspondents filing from distant datelines were regularly required to file audio tracks for sequences of images they had never seen.

Silent fix. To turn a green story red for an instant in order to fix something wrong or infelicitous without going through the rigmarole and potential embarrassment of re-publishing it as a **Corrected Version**. Silent fixes messed with the integrity of the **ENPS** system but if they were done quickly no harm was done. Ahem.

Smithfield. The London meat market within walking distance of Bush

House where a few pubs stayed open all night, thereby affording the Newsroom's night shift an opportunity for a quick drink before going home.

Snap. A quick-fire story of one or two sentences, the first stage of breaking news.

Sources. The written source material for every story (usually newswire copy and/or BBC correspondents' despatches) had to be identified by its writer at the bottom of each story. These sources had to be updated every time the story was re-written such that anyone reading it for the first time could work out exactly how old it was and what had been done to it.

Spanish practices. A newspaper term derived from the printing trades. Turning up late or leaving early were the most common Spanish practices in the Newsroom especially at weekends when there were no bosses around.

Spike. To spike a story was to reject it for consideration. In the days before computers, the **SDE** had a metal spike on his or her desk on which he or she impaled rejected **copy**. The phrase remained in colloquial use thereafter as a term for decisive action. "Didn't you do anything with that Somalia story?" "Nah. The Somalis said it was rubbish so I spiked it."

Storify. The Newsroom verb for turning a **snap** into a proper story with a time slug, a title, **sources** and a **net head.**

Tail. Centre Desk's one-minute written news summary, matching the headlines in the **Top.**

Talkback. A computer folder attached to the **Newsroom Log** in which staff could raise questions or make comments relating to Newsroom procedures and matters of style.

Tape. News from a news agency. Derived from the pre-digital days when all news agencies filed their copy on teleprinter machines fed by fat rolls of newspaper tape. In the BBC, 'tape' also referred to anything recoded on an actual length of audio or video tape, which sometimes led to confusion.

Top. The Centre Desk's headlines, usually three items with an optional one in brackets.

Touch base. As a noun, the morning departmental meeting of WSNCA held in the Editor's office at about 0940 hours (after the Bush House 0900 editorial meeting held in **Centre Block**). As a verb, to chat to someone about a matter of concern. As in, "Can we touch base later today to talk about your appraisal?"

Third Floor. The home base of World Service Current Affairs programmes in English. The advent of 24-hour news led to a considerable expansion of activity on the Third Floor, with a proportionate increase in its budget.

Used Tape Box. A much bashed about piece of joinery for containing the source material of every story written in the Newsroom. Centre Desk's guiding principle was that every story had to be based on at least two independent **sources**.

Wire. A news agency. In the old days it sent its news down a wire.

WOODS. Working On Off Days. BBC jargon for overtime. Staff working a WOODS could either be paid for it or ask for it to be credited as extra leave.